AF657075

The Happiness Trap Pocketbook

Stop Struggling, Start Living: An Illustrated Guide

Dr Russ Harris
&
Bev Aisbett

PAN

First published 2016 by Pan
an imprint of Pan Macmillan India,
a division of Macmillan Publishers India Private Limited
707, Kailash Building
26 KG Marg, New Delhi 110001
www.panmacmillan.co.in

Pan Macmillan, the Smithson, 6 Briset St, London EC1M 5NR, United Kingdom
Basingstoke and Oxford
Associated companies throughout the world
www.panmacmillan.com

ISBN 978-93-82616-77-1
Text copyright © Russ Harris 2016
Illustrations copyright © Bev Aisbett 2016

All rights reserved. No part of this publication may be reproduced, stored in or introduced into a retrieval system, or transmitted, in any form, or by any means (electronic, mechanical, photocopying, recording or otherwise) without the prior written permission of the publisher. Any person who does any unauthorized act in relation to this publication may be liable to criminal prosecution and civil claims for damages.

3 5 7 9 8 6 4 2

This book is sold subject to the condition that it shall not, by way of trade or otherwise, be lent, re-sold, hired out, or otherwise circulated without the publisher's prior consent in any form of binding or cover other than that in which it is published and without a similar condition including this condition being imposed on the subsequent purchaser.

Typeset by Manmohan Kumar
Printed and bound in India by Repro India Ltd

Contents

The Happiness Trap Pocketbook

Dr Russ Harris is a medical practitioner, psychotherapist and executive coach. He grew up in the UK, but moved to Australia in his early twenties and now lives in Melbourne. He is the author of seven books, including the bestselling *The Happiness Trap* and *The Reality Slap*. A world-renowned trainer in Acceptance and Commitment Therapy, he has so far trained 14,000 health professionals in the approach.

Bev Aisbett is an accomplished author, illustrator and exhibiting artist. Her illustrated self-help books have gained prominence with both readers and health professionals as invaluable guides to overcoming anxiety and depression, eating disorders, self-esteem issues and releasing past trauma. Since 1998, Bev has facilitated her anxiety recovery program and her work has reached thousands of sufferers through her lectures, interviews and training sessions.

Also by Dr Russ Harris

The Happiness Trap

How to use this book

Welcome to *The Happiness Trap Pocketbook*, an illustrated and simplified version of the international bestseller, *The Happiness Trap*. There are at least three ways you could use this book:

1. **As an easy-to-read introduction to Acceptance & Commitment Therapy**

This book presents a delightfully easy introduction to the main ideas of Acceptance & Commitment Therapy (better known as ACT). We see it as especially useful for people who are not really into reading traditional self-help books, or for those who are so stressed, anxious or depressed that reading is difficult. Of course, we hope that you will then go on to read the original book, which explores ACT in far greater depth.

2. **As an adjunct to coaching or therapy**

If you are seeing a coach or therapist who uses the ACT approach, this book can be a valuable adjunct. You can read chapters ahead of time to prepare for a session, or after a session as a reminder.

3. **As a quick refresher course**

If it's been a while since you read *The Happiness Trap*, you can use the pocketbook as a quick refresher course to remind yourself of the main ideas and exercises.

An Important Message

Simply reading this book will not be enough to make any real difference in your life. You actually will need to do the exercises if you want your life to be richer, fuller and more meaningful. It is much the same as reading a book on how to play tennis or guitar. Your tennis or guitar skills won't improve simply from reading it; you actually have to do the recommended exercises.

Of course, you can read through the book quickly and then go back and do the exercises, but it's far better to do them as you go.

So, good luck with it all. And remember: life gives most to those who make the most of what life gives.

Cheers
Russ Harris

Introduction

If you're HAPPY and you know it,
CLAP YOUR HANDS...
OH DEAR!

We should be HAPPY, shouldn't we?

That's what the multitude of self-help books out there suggest – just think happy thoughts and you'll be FINE. But trying to be perpetually positive can be downright STRESSFUL!

MY DOG DIED, I LOST MY JOB, MY WIFE LEFT ME ... BUT IT'S ALL *GOOD*!

BUT ISN'T IT *NORMAL* TO BE HAPPY?

You'd think that it would be normal to be happy in the western world, where we have access to so many of the ingredients to build happiness...

GOOD HOUSING

MORE & BETTER FOOD

EXCELLENT MEDICAL FACILITIES

ACCESS TO

EDUCATION

JUSTICE

WELFARE

CLEAN WATER & SANITATION

Along with FREEDOM TO

TRAVEL

SPEAK OPENLY

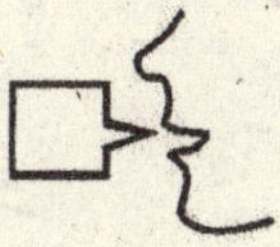

VOTE

But the truth is, on the whole we're NOT happy.
In fact, often we're downright MISERABLE!

Here are some sobering statistics:

1 in 10 has CLINICAL DEPRESSION

1 in 5 is DEPRESSED at some time

1 in 4 has or has had an ADDICTION

30 per cent of the adult population has a recognised PSYCHOLOGICAL DISORDER

And of all the people you know, almost HALF of these will **SERIOUSLY CONTEMPLATE SUICIDE** at some point...

...and 1 in 10 will actually ATTEMPT IT!

SO WHY IS IT SO *DIFFICULT* TO BE HAPPY?
TO ANSWER THAT, WE NEED TO GO BACK IN TIME TO SEE HOW OUR MINDS *EVOLVED*!
HANG ON!
WOW!!
HERE'S AN EARLY HUNTER/GATHERER. WHAT DO YOU THINK ARE HIS *NEEDS*?
HMM ... WELL, THE *BASICS* FOR SURVIVAL!
FOOD
WATER
SHELTER
SEX
AND HE HAS AN EVEN *GREATER* PRIORITY!
DON'T GET KILLED!

THE BETTER WE WERE ABLE TO ANTICIPATE AND AVOID DANGER, THE BETTER OUR CHANCES OF SURVIVAL!
GOOD? BAD? HELPFUL?
TRUE, BUT THERE AREN'T ANY SABRE-TOOTHED TIGERS IN MY SUBURB! WHAT'S THIS GOT TO DO WITH MODERN-DAY HAPPINESS?
WELL, LOOK AT HOW WE'VE 'EVOLVED'! COMPARE THE 'DANGERS' ON OUR ANCESTORS' LIST TO OUR CURRENT PERCEIVED 'DANGERS' — MOST OF WHICH WON'T EVEN HAPPEN!
SO I GUESS WE'VE JUST EVOLVED TO BE BETTER AT LOOKING FOR TROUBLE!
PREDATORS
BAD WEATHER
ILLNESS
LACK OF FOOD OR WATER
MORTGAGE REJECTION JOB
EMBARRASSMENT LOSS
WAR
UPSETTING LOVED ONES
BANKRUPTCY
PAYING BILLS
THEFT
SPEEDING TICKET
Climate Change
POLLUTION
GETTING CANCER
ATTACK
OBESITY DRUGS STUFF

WHAT DO YOU THINK WAS THE GREATEST THREAT TO SURVIVAL FOR OUR FRIEND HERE?
LET'S SEE ... WELL, BEING ALONE WOULD BE DANGEROUS, I GUESS!
YES! WITHOUT THE PROTECTION OF THE TRIBE, HE WOULD BE EASY PREY!
SO HOW DOES THIS PLAY OUT IN MODERN TIMES?
WE STILL FEAR REJECTION AND TRY TO 'PROTECT' OURSELVES BY COMPARING OURSELVES TO OTHERS!
AM I FITTING IN?
AM I DOING ANYTHING WRONG?
AM I AS GOOD AS OTHERS?

AND BACK THEN, THERE WAS ONLY A SMALL GROUP TO COMPARE TO!
NOW IT'S *GLOBAL*!
RICHER
SMARTER
FAMOUS
SEXIER
FOR AN AMBITIOUS ANCESTOR THE FORMULA FOR SUCCESS WAS *MORE = BETTER*
WELL THAT SURE HASN'T *CHANGED*!
AND IT SEEMS THAT NO MATTER HOW MUCH WE GET, WE STILL WANT MORE!
YES! OUR MODERN MINDS TEND TO FOCUS ON *LACK* & CREATE DISSATISFACTION!

SO WHAT IS THIS HAPPINESS THAT WE KEEP CHASING AFTER?

'The very purpose of life is to seek Happiness.'
Dalai Lama

'HAPPINESS' HAS TWO VERY DIFFERENT MEANINGS...

1.

A GOOD FEELING

Because happiness feels GOOD, we CHASE it, but we find that it doesn't LAST.

And, as we shall see, a life spent chasing after this feeling is not only UNSATISFACTORY but also the harder we try to experience only pleasurable feelings, the more we feel ANXIOUS or DEPRESSED when they elude us.

2. AN ACTIVE PHILOSOPHY

THIS SECOND DEFINITION INSTEAD FOCUSES ON CREATING ***A RICH, FULL & MEANINGFUL*** LIFE!

This involves...

TAKING ACTION ON THE THINGS THAT MATTER TO US

MOVING IN THE DIRECTION OF WHAT WE SEE AS VALUABLE OR WORTHY

ENGAGING FULLY IN WHAT WE DO

IN DOING SO, WE EMBRACE LIFE IN ***ALL*** ITS COLOURS!

But a full human life comes with the FULL RANGE of human emotions.

OF COURSE WE ALL LIKE TO FEEL *GOOD*, BUT DESPERATELY TRYING TO AVOID PAINFUL FEELINGS DOOMS US TO *FAILURE*.

The fact is – life involves PAIN:

LOSS — SEPARATION OR DIVORCE — REJECTION — ILLNESS OR INFIRMITY

THE GOOD NEWS IS...

You can learn to handle painful feelings by:

- MAKING ROOM FOR THEM
- RISING ABOVE THEM
- CREATING A LIFE WORTH LIVING.

AND WE'LL SHOW YOU HOW, USING THE PRINCIPLES OF *ACT: ACCEPTANCE AND COMMITMENT THERAPY.*

Chapter 1

Fairytales

...AND THEY LIVED *HAPPILY EVER AFTER*...
WE'LL ALL LIVE HAPPILY EVER AFTER, WON'T WE MUMMY?

HAPPY ENDINGS ... we believe that's how life should be, don't we? Is this REALISTIC? Does this fit with your own experience of life?

HMMM...
DISEASE
MONEY WORRIES
JOB LOSS
HEART BREAK
GLOBAL WARMING
STRESS
LOSS

An expectation that life should turn out 'happily ever after' is one of the ways that we find ourselves caught in the **HAPPINESS TRAP**.

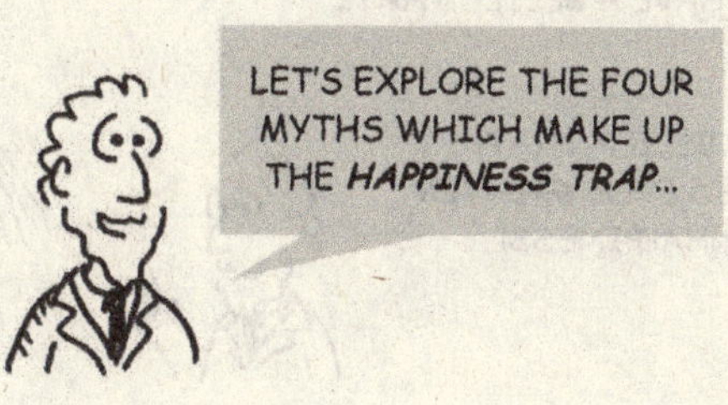
LET'S EXPLORE THE FOUR MYTHS WHICH MAKE UP THE *HAPPINESS TRAP*...

MYTH 1: HAPPINESS IS THE NATURAL STATE FOR HUMAN BEINGS

Our culture insists that humans are naturally happy. Yet, the scary statistics regarding mental illness in the introduction to this book tell another story.

And aside from diagnosed psychiatric disorders, there are things like:

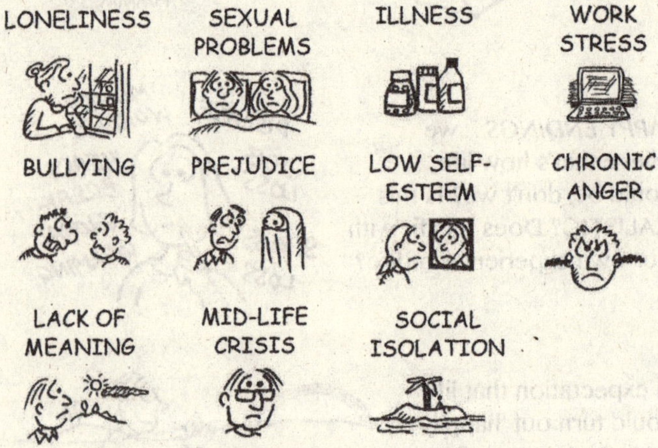
LONELINESS
SEXUAL PROBLEMS
ILLNESS
WORK STRESS
BULLYING
PREJUDICE
LOW SELF-ESTEEM
CHRONIC ANGER
LACK OF MEANING
MID-LIFE CRISIS
SOCIAL ISOLATION

SO LASTING HAPPINESS IS ACTUALLY QUITE *RARE*, YET MANY OF US HAVE A BELIEF THAT...
EVERYONE IS HAPPY EXCEPT *ME*!
...A BELIEF THAT CREATES EVEN *GREATER* UNHAPPINESS!

MYTH 2: IF YOU'RE NOT HAPPY, YOU'RE DEFECTIVE

I MUST BE REALLY *MESSED UP*!

Our society tends to assume that psychological suffering is ABNORMAL: a sign of a WEAKNESS or ILLNESS and a mind that is FAULTY or DEFECTIVE.

YOU SHOULDN'T BE FEELING SO ANXIOUS.
OH NO! I MUST BE *MENTALLY ILL*!

This means that, when we inevitably experience painful thoughts and feelings, we BEAT UP on ourselves for doing so.

I'M *WEAK*!
I'M *STUPID*!

BUT AS YOU WILL SEE, YOUR MIND IS JUST DOING THE JOB IT HAS *EVOLVED* TO DO!

ACT PRINCIPLE:

THE ***NORMAL*** THINKING PROCESSES OF A ***HEALTHY*** MIND NATURALLY CREATE PSYCHOLOGICAL SUFFERING!

MYTH 3:
TO CREATE A BETTER LIFE, WE MUST GET RID OF NEGATIVE FEELINGS

The current trend of a 'feel-good' society tells us to ELIMINATE 'negative' feelings and ACCUMULATE the 'positive'.

But in reality, the things we value most in life give rise to a whole RANGE of feelings – PLEASANT and UNPLEASANT.

For instance, in a long-term relationship, there may be JOY...

...but also FRUSTRATION.

Anything that's MEANINGFUL in our lives will bring with it... both pleasure *and* pain!

Living life to the full means experiencing UNCOMFORTABLE FEELINGS along the way. Learning how to HANDLE these feelings is essential.

MYTH 4:
YOU SHOULD BE ABLE TO CONTROL WHAT YOU THINK AND FEEL

Many current self-help programs subscribe to this myth by:

REPLACING 'NEGATIVE' THOUGHTS WITH 'POSITIVE' ONES

DOING AFFIRMATIONS...

EVERYTHING IS
HUNKY-DORY!

...OR VISUALISATIONS

$ ♥ ☆

The basic theme behind these approaches is:

'THINK HAPPY THOUGHTS AND YOU'LL BE HAPPY'.

If only life was that SIMPLE! Over one hundred thousand years of evolution tend to override a few affirmations!

Even though you might be able to master positive thinking when you are relatively CALM, negative thoughts will start to creep in again when you feel STRESSED.

ANGER
SADNESS
INSECURITY
GUILT
LA LA LA
HAPPY
HAPPY

They go away, then they're back. They go away, then they're back – and the battle to keep them at bay can be STRESSFUL in itself!

AARGH!
CAN'T BE
SAD/
ANGRY/
UPSET!

These four basic myths set us up for a battle we can NEVER WIN.

SO ARE YOU SAYING THAT NEGATIVE THOUGHTS AND FEELINGS ARE *NORMAL*?
YES. LIFE INVOLVES *PAIN*.
THEN HOW DID THESE MYTHS BECOME SO *ENTRENCHED* IN OUR CULTURE?
BECAUSE WE HAVE SO MUCH *CONTROL* OVER THE MATERIAL WORLD WE EXPECT TO HAVE *CONTROL* OVER OUR INTERNAL WORLD, BUT THIS IS *UNREALISTIC*.
TRY THESE EXPERIMENTS AND YOU'LL *SEE*!

1. DON'T THINK ABOUT ICE-CREAM FOR 30 SECONDS. DON'T THINK ABOUT ITS COLOUR, TEXTURE OR TASTE.

DON'T THINK ABOUT IT! *DAMN*!

2. LOOK AT THIS STAR FOR ONE MINUTE, BUT AS YOU DO, DON'T THINK ABOUT IT!

DAMN!

3. IMAGINE SOMEONE POINTS A GUN AT YOUR HEAD, AND SAYS 'YOU MUST FEEL NO ANXIETY – OR I WILL SHOOT YOU!'

I GUESS IT WOULD BE *CURTAINS* FOR ME!

4. CONJURE UP A MEMORY. NOW FORGET IT.

CAN'T.

5. FEEL THE INSIDE OF YOUR MOUTH. NOW MAKE IT NUMB.

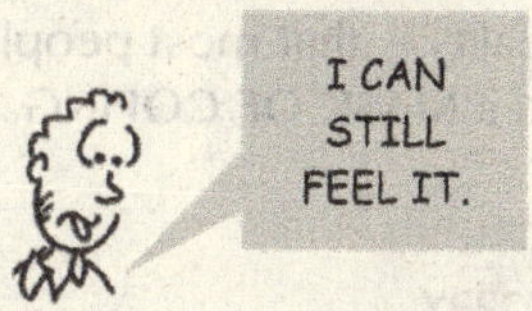
I CAN STILL FEEL IT.

From an early age, we are taught that we should be able to CONTROL OUR FEELINGS:

DON'T CRY
STOP FROWNING
STOP FEELING SORRY FOR YOURSELF
THERE'S NO NEED TO BE SCARED

And this is REINFORCED as we get older.

YOU BIG SISSY!
CHILL OUT!
SNAP OUT OF IT!
DON'T BE SUCH A CHICKEN!

The implication is that you should be able to flick a switch and turn your feelings on or off at WILL.

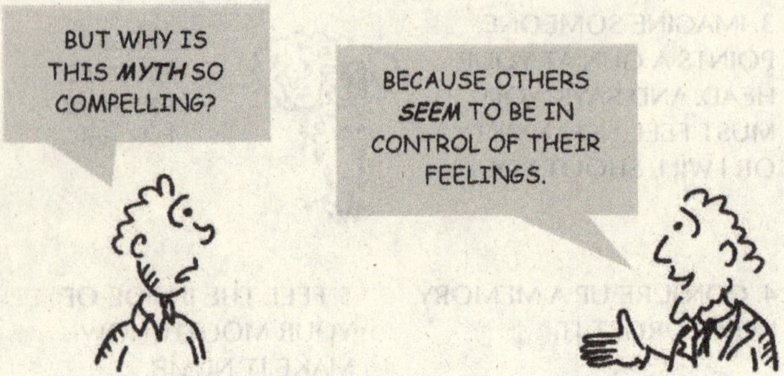
BUT WHY IS THIS *MYTH* SO COMPELLING?
BECAUSE OTHERS *SEEM* TO BE IN CONTROL OF THEIR FEELINGS.

The reality is that most people hide their inner struggles behind a MASK OF COPING...

WORRY WORRY WORRY
NO *WORRIES MATE*!

...and this false front adds to the ILLUSION of CONTROL.

Chapter 2

Vicious cycles

What's happening in your life?

I HAVE RELATIONSHIP PROBLEMS!
I HATE MY JOB!
I'M LONELY.
I HAVE HEALTH ISSUES.
I FEEL REJECTED.
I'VE LOST CONFIDENCE!
I'M AN ADDICT!
I'M IN FINANCIAL CRISIS!
I'M JUST STUCK!
I'M ANXIOUS!
I'M DEPRESSED!
WELL I HAVE EVERYTHING I NEED BUT I'M UNHAPPY.

Whatever the problem is, it gives rise to UNPLEASANT THOUGHTS and FEELINGS which you try to GET RID OF.

I'VE TRIED TO *IGNORE* THEM!
I'VE TRIED TO *ELIMINATE* THEM!
I'VE TRIED TO *BLOT* THEM *OUT*!
THESE ATTEMPTS TO GET RID OF UNWANTED FEELINGS ARE MAKING THEM *WORSE*!
WHAT DO YOU MEAN?

The more you try to GET RID OF, AVOID or ESCAPE feelings, the BIGGER they become.

I'M AFRAID OF REJECTION.
AND IF I SOCIALISE I MIGHT BE REJECTED!
SO I AVOID SOCIAL SITUATIONS.
SO I FEEL EVEN *MORE* REJECTED!

ALCOHOL HELPS ME COPE WITH MY SOCIAL ANXIETY!
OH NO! DID I REALLY DO THAT LAST NIGHT?
AND I SPENT ALL THAT MONEY!
I'M TOO ASHAMED TO FACE ANYONE!
CHOCOLATE CHEERS ME UP!
TEMPORARILY!
WEIGH IN
YOU'RE ALWAYS WORKING! WHY DON'T YOU STAY HOME WITH ME?
IT'S SO TENSE AT HOME!
WHERE ARE YOU?!
I HAD TO DO OVERTIME AGAIN!

We have two main ways of trying to avoid painful thoughts and feelings: FIGHT or FLIGHT.

FIGHT

Trying to fight against unwanted thoughts/ feelings by:

SUPPRESSION

You forcefully push away unwanted thoughts or unwanted feelings deep inside.

ARGUING WITH YOURSELF

YOU'RE A FAILURE!
NO I'M NOT!

You attempt to challenge and disprove negative thoughts.

FLIGHT

Running away or hiding from unwanted thoughts/ feelings by:

HIDING/ESCAPING

You avoid situations in which you feel uncomfortable.

DISTRACTION

You focus on something else to avoid unwanted thoughts and feelings.

TAKING CHARGE

SNAP OUT OF IT!
STAY CALM!
CHEER UP!

You try to force yourself to feel better.

SELF-BULLYING

IDIOT!
DON'T BE SO
PATHETIC!

You beat yourself up for having these thoughts/ feelings.

ZONING OUT/ NUMBING

You make yourself 'unconscious' to the thoughts/feelings.

PILLS AND DRUGS

You use medication, alcohol or drugs to escape the pain.

BUT WHAT'S WRONG WITH THESE THINGS IF THEY HELP YOU TO *COPE*?
NOTHING – IF YOU USE THEM...

- IN MODERATION
- WHEN THEY CAN ACTUALLY WORK
- IF THEY DON'T STOP YOU DOING THE THINGS YOU VALUE.

For example, DISTRACTING YOURSELF after an argument or a tough day can be helpful...

I NEED SOME *TIME* OUT!

...but if you spend ALL NIGHT distracting yourself you'll miss out on LIFE!

THE BORING & THE BLAH

Any method to avoid pain, if used excessively will create GREATER PROBLEMS:

AAH! *CHOCOLATE*!

OOH AH! *DIABETES*!
M.D.

I'LL TAKE MY MIND OFF THIS *EXAM* STRESS!

F

Trying to BURY deep pain doesn't make it DISAPPEAR!

I CAN'T *FACE* THE GRIEF!
SO I'LL *AVOID* IT!
BUT IT KEEPS *COMING BACK*!
SO I HAVE TO DO *MORE* TO AVOID IT!

Avoiding painful feelings can stop you doing what you VALUE:

I LOVE ACTING!
BUT I FEEL SO *ANXIOUS*!
SO NO MORE ACTING FOR ME!
TONITE PLAYS FOR PEOPLE

SO HOW MUCH *CONTROL* DO WE REALLY HAVE OVER OUR FEELINGS?
IT DEPENDS ON THEIR INTENSITY AND THE IMPORTANCE OF THE SITUATION.

A simple RELAXATION TECHNIQUE may be enough to ease a stressful day at WORK...

RELAX AND BREATHE...

...but it won't do much for OUTRIGHT TERROR!

RELAX?! ARE YOU *KIDDING*?!

AND WHILE YOU MIGHT BE ABLE TO SIMPLY *IGNORE* A MESSY ROOM...

...IT'S HARD TO IGNORE A SINISTER LUMP!

SO HOW DOES THAT FIT WITH THE *HAPPINESS TRAP*?

THE TRAP IS THAT TRYING TO AVOID PAINFUL FEELINGS IS MOSTLY *INEFFECTIVE*...

- IT TAKES A LOT OF TIME AND ENERGY
- WE FEEL INADEQUATE WHEN THE UNWANTED THOUGHTS/FEELINGS COME BACK
- IT OFTEN HAS LONG-TERM COSTS TO WELLBEING.

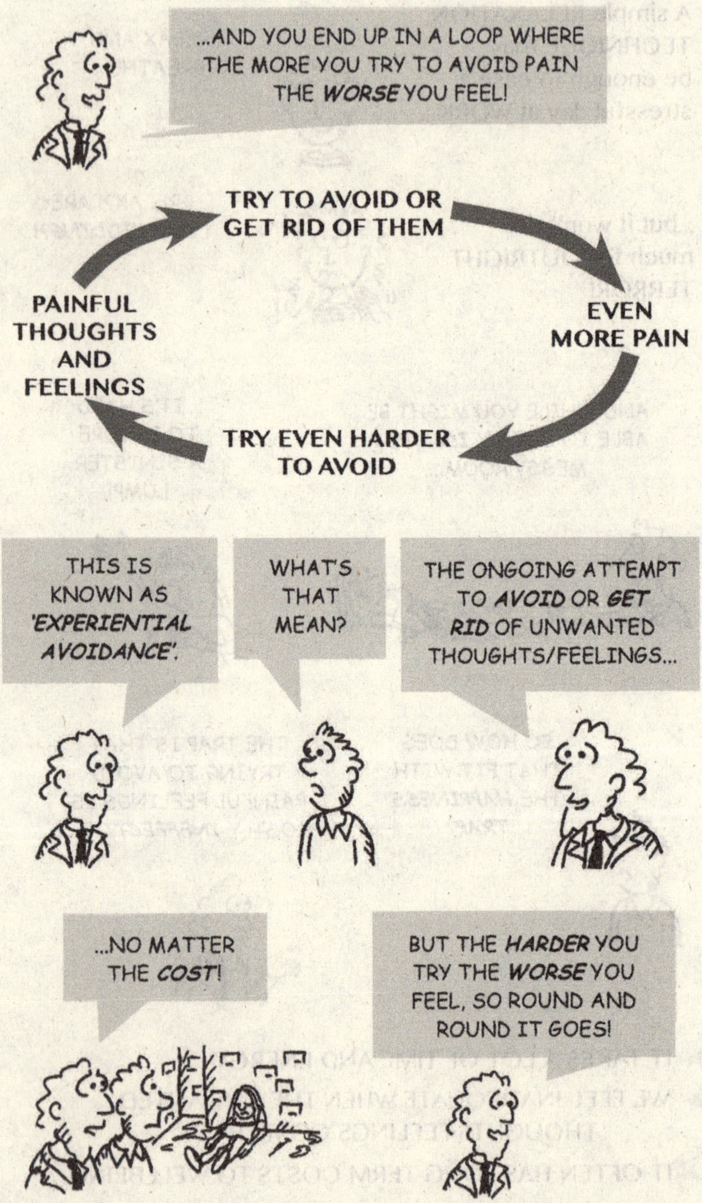
...AND YOU END UP IN A LOOP WHERE THE MORE YOU TRY TO AVOID PAIN THE *WORSE* YOU FEEL!
TRY TO AVOID OR GET RID OF THEM
EVEN MORE PAIN
TRY EVEN HARDER TO AVOID
PAINFUL THOUGHTS AND FEELINGS
THIS IS KNOWN AS *'EXPERIENTIAL AVOIDANCE'*.
WHAT'S THAT MEAN?
THE ONGOING ATTEMPT TO *AVOID* OR *GET RID* OF UNWANTED THOUGHTS/FEELINGS...
...NO MATTER THE *COST*!
BUT THE *HARDER* YOU TRY THE *WORSE* YOU FEEL, SO ROUND AND ROUND IT GOES!

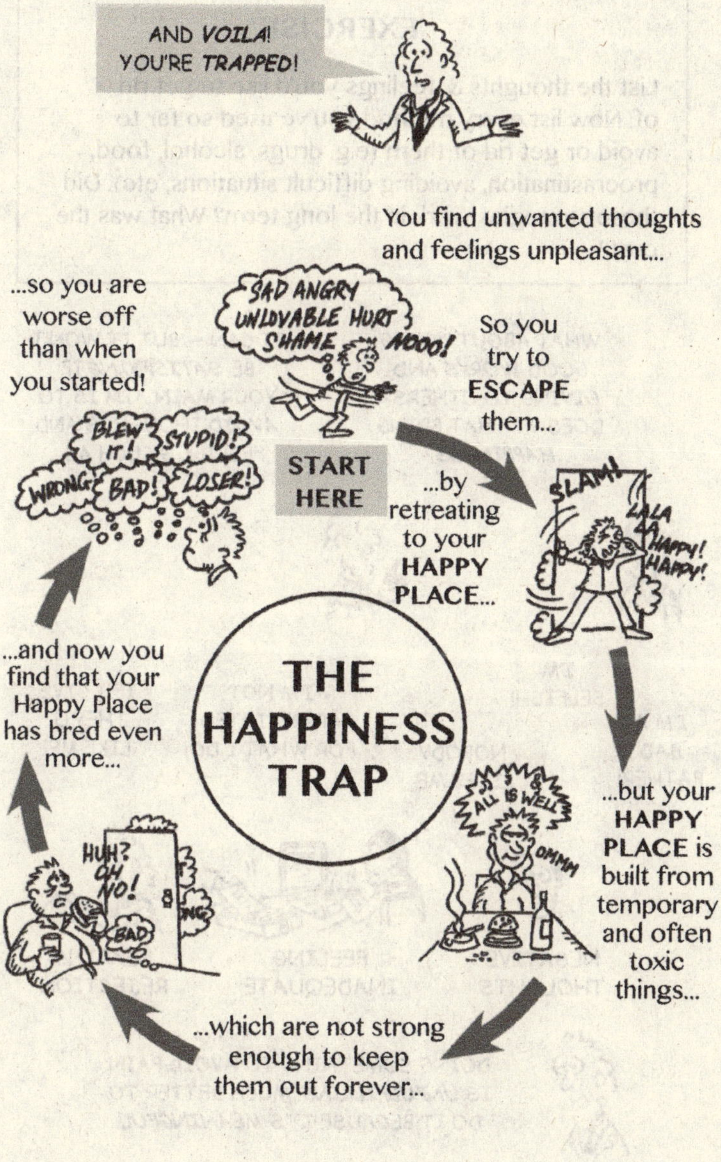
THE HAPPINESS TRAP
START HERE
SAD ANGRY UNLOVABLE HURT SHAME
NOOO!
You find unwanted thoughts and feelings unpleasant...
So you try to ESCAPE them...
...by retreating to your HAPPY PLACE...
SLAM!
LALA LA HAPPY! HAPPY!
...but your HAPPY PLACE is built from temporary and often toxic things...
ALL IS WELL
OMMM
...which are not strong enough to keep them out forever...
HUH? OH NO!
BAD
...and now you find that your Happy Place has bred even more...
BLEW IT! STUPID!
WRONG BAD! LOSER!
...so you are worse off than when you started!
AND VOILA! YOU'RE TRAPPED!

EXERCISE

List the thoughts & feelings you'd like to get rid of. Now list every method you've used so far to avoid or get rid of them (e.g. drugs, alcohol, food, procrastination, avoiding difficult situations, etc). Did these strategies work in the long term? What was the cost?

WHAT ABOUT DOING GOOD *WORKS* AND GIVING TO OTHERS? DOESN'T THAT BRING *HAPPINESS*?
IT CAN — BUT IT WON'T BE *SATISFYING* IF YOUR MAIN AIM IS TO *AVOID* THOUGHTS AND FEELINGS SUCH AS...
I'M A BAD FATHER!
I'M SELFISH!
NOBODY LIKES ME.
I'M NOT APPRECIATED FOR WHAT I DO!
IF I GIVE THEY'LL LIKE ME!
NEGATIVE THOUGHTS
FEELING INADEQUATE
FEARING REJECTION
DOING SOMETHING TO AVOID PAIN IS *UNFULFILLING*. MUCH BETTER TO DO IT BECAUSE IT'S *MEANINGFUL*!

Consider running through a forest. You can run through a forest to MEET YOUR LOVER.

You can run through a forest to ESCAPE A BEAR.

When we do any activity primarily to escape or avoid something unwanted, it is usually unfulfilling, because it feels like we are on the run from something, rather than doing something meaningful. Of course, we are not usually on the run from wild animals, but rather from painful thoughts and feelings.

Likewise you can go to the gym to look after and TAKE CARE OF YOUR BODY.

Or you can go to the gym to ESCAPE UNPLEASANT THOUGHTS OR FEELINGS.

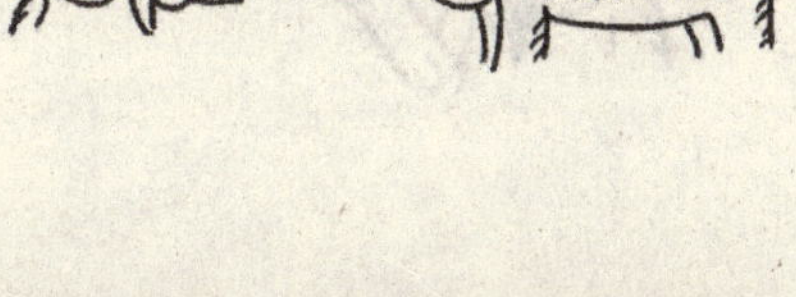
I'M FAT
BIG THIGHS
I'M
UNATTRACTIVE

You'll hear a lot of ADVICE on how to IMPROVE YOUR LIFE:

GET FIT!
MAKE NEW FRIENDS!
GET OUT IN NATURE!
JOIN A CLUB!
EAT RIGHT!
GET A MEANINGFUL JOB!
TAKE UP A HOBBY!

But be warned: if you start doing any of these things primarily to ESCAPE or AVOID unpleasant feelings, it probably won't be rewarding. Better to do things because they are genuinely important and meaningful, rather than to try to avoid pain.

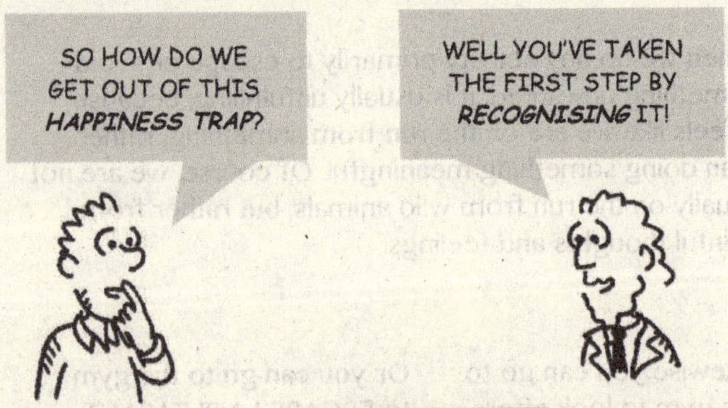
SO HOW DO WE GET OUT OF THIS HAPPINESS TRAP?
WELL YOU'VE TAKEN THE FIRST STEP BY RECOGNISING IT!

NOW IT'S TIME TO MOVE ON TO APPROPRIATE ACTION!

Chapter 3

The basics of ACT

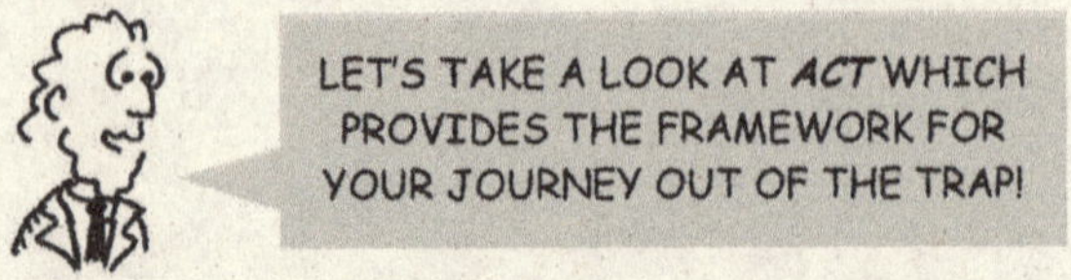
LET'S TAKE A LOOK AT *ACT* WHICH PROVIDES THE FRAMEWORK FOR YOUR JOURNEY OUT OF THE TRAP!

***ACT* – ACCEPTANCE and COMMITMENT THERAPY** – is based on two main principles: 'mindfulness' and 'values'. These principles work together to help you:

- **EFFECTIVELY HANDLE PAINFUL THOUGHTS AND FEELINGS**
- **CREATE A RICH, FULL AND MEANINGFUL LIFE.**

'Mindfulness' is a special mental state of AWARENESS and OPENNESS. Mindfulness involves three skills:

SKILL 1: DEFUSION

When you learn to defuse painful and unpleasant thoughts, self-limiting beliefs and self-criticism, they have less influence over you.

SKILL 2: EXPANSION

This means 'making room' for painful thoughts and feelings and allowing them to flow through you, without getting swept away by them.

SKILL 3: CONNECTION

NOW!

This means living fully in the present instead of dwelling on the past or worrying about the future.

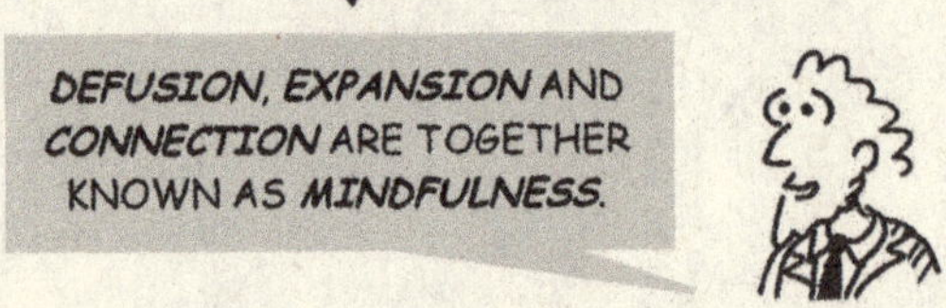
DEFUSION, *EXPANSION* AND *CONNECTION* ARE TOGETHER KNOWN AS *MINDFULNESS*.

'Values' are your heart's deepest desires for how you want to behave as a human being; what you want to STAND FOR in life.

In ***ACT***, you use 'values' to give life MEANING, PURPOSE and DIRECTION.

I
DID
IT!

And you translate values into COMMITTED ACTION: you do what really matters to you!

ACT is a scientifically proven method to help you build a RICHER, FULLER and more MEANINGFUL life.
Are you ready to GET MOVING? Let's go!

ONE STEP
AT A TIME!

Chapter 4

The great storyteller

NOW WE'RE GOING TO LOOK AT HOW TO HANDLE OUR *THOUGHTS.*
WHAT *ARE* THOUGHTS EXACTLY?
THOUGHTS ARE BASICALLY *WORDS.*
WORDS?

We use words in different settings...

WORDS ON A PAGE ARE CALLED **TEXT:**

WORDS SPOKEN OUT LOUD ARE CALLED **SPEECH:**

AND WORDS INSIDE OUR HEAD ARE CALLED **THOUGHTS:**

The quick brown fox jumps over the lazy dog.
YAKKITY YAK
BLAH BLAH BLAH

Thoughts can also be IMAGES:

WORDS **IMAGE**

BREAKFAST! I'LL HAVE TOAST AND JAM!

But please don't confuse THOUGHTS with 'FEELINGS' or 'SENSATIONS' – which we feel in the BODY.

We'll explore FEELINGS and SENSATIONS later. Let's stick with THOUGHTS for now.

THOUGHTS – TELL US ABOUT LIFE & HOW TO LIVE IT... ...HOW WE ARE OR SHOULD BE AND WHAT TO AVOID.

What we tend to forget is that thoughts are just words which constitute our 'stories'.

These can be TRUE stories called **FACTS**... ...or FALSE stories.

But most stories are based on how we see life according to our... or what we want to do with our lives:

THE HUMAN MIND IS LIKE A STORYTELLING MACHINE. ALL IT WANTS IS OUR *ATTENTION*!
BLAH, BLAH, BLAH, STORY, STORY, STORY, GIVE ME YOUR ATTENTION!
BUT IF WE GET TOO *CAUGHT UP* IN THESE STORIES, IT CREATES PROBLEMS:
BAD THINGS WILL HAPPEN!
I'M NOT *GOOD ENOUGH*.
HOW *DARE* THEY?!
I *CAN'T* DO IT!

WHEN A STORY *DOMINATES* US — WHEN IT CAPTURES OUR FULL ATTENTION OR DICTATES HOW WE BEHAVE — WE REFER TO THIS AS *FUSION*.
NOW HERE'S AN *AMAZING FACT*...
NEWS FLASH!
NO THOUGHT IS PROBLEMATIC IN AND OF ITSELF. OUR THOUGHTS ONLY BECOME PROBLEMATIC IF WE 'FUSE' WITH THEM!
REALLY?
SURE! IN A MOMENT YOU'LL SEE THAT NO MATTER HOW *NEGATIVE* A THOUGHT IS, IT'S ONLY PROBLEMATIC IF YOU *FUSE* WITH IT!
I DON'T UNDERSTAND!

THIS WILL MAKE IT CLEARER. JOT DOWN SOME OF YOUR NEGATIVE THOUGHTS ON A SHEET OF PAPER.
OKAY.
I'M NOT GOOD ENOUGH I'M FAT
NOW HOLD THE PAPER IN FRONT OF YOUR FACE AND GET ALL ABSORBED IN THOSE WORDS.
I'M A BAD MOTHER I'M A LOSER I'M STUPID
WHILE YOU'RE ALL CAUGHT UP IN THESE THOUGHTS YOU ARE *CUT OFF* OR *DISCONNECTED* FROM THE THINGS THAT MAKE LIFE *MEANINGFUL*.
I'M NOT SMART ENOUGH LIFE SUCKS!
LIFE SUCKS

AND WHILE YOU'RE HOLDING ON TIGHTLY TO THESE THOUGHTS, IT'S HARD TO DO THE THINGS THAT MAKE YOUR LIFE WORK!
IMAGINE TRYING TO COOK DINNER, DRIVE A CAR, CUDDLE A BABY OR WATCH A MOVIE WHEN YOU'RE DOING THIS!
I'M NOT GOOD ENOUGH
WHEN WE FUSE WITH OUR THOUGHTS THEY SEEM TO BE...

▶ **THE TRUTH**	You should BELIEVE THEM!
▶ **IMPORTANT**	You should give them your FULL ATTENTION!
▶ **ORDERS**	You must OBEY them!
▶ **GREAT ADVICE**	You should do what they SUGGEST!
▶ **THREATS**	They are DANGEROUS or FRIGHTENING.

NOW TUCK THAT SHEET OF PAPER UNDER YOUR ARM...
...AND NOTICE THAT NOW YOU CAN *CONNECT* AND *ENGAGE* WITH THE THINGS THAT MAKE LIFE *MEANINGFUL*!
FOOD
MUSIC
FRIENDS & FAMILY
SPORT
WORK
CHILDREN
MOVIES
WHEN YOU DO THIS WITH YOUR THOUGHTS WE CALL IT *DEFUSION*.
CAN YOU SHOW ME *HOW*?
SURE. FIRST, BRING TO MIND A *NEGATIVE SELF-JUDGEMENT*...
I'M *USELESS*!
...NOW *FUSE* WITH IT — *BELIEVE* IT AS MUCH AS YOU CAN.
I'M *USELESS*!

NOW INSERT THIS PHRASE IN FRONT OF IT – 'I'M HAVING THE THOUGHT THAT...'
I'M HAVING THE THOUGHT THAT I'M USELESS!

EXERCISE

Pick an upsetting thought, and silently repeat it, putting these words in front of it: 'I'm having the thought that...'

Now try it again with this phrase: '*I notice I'm having the thought that...*'

Can you feel the thought lose some of its impact?

You can use this simple defusion technique to unhook yourself from any thought, whether true or false – so please play around it.

When we defuse from our thoughts we realise they:

- are nothing more or less than WORDS and PICTURES
- may or may not be TRUE (we don't have to BELIEVE them)
- may or may not be IMPORTANT (we pay attention only if they're helpful)
- are not ORDERS (we don't have to obey!)
- may or may not be WISE – we don't have to follow the advice
- are never actual THREATS, no matter how negative.

SO LET'S *DEFUSE* ANOTHER TROUBLESOME THOUGHT. GOT ONE?
YEP!
I'M A LOSER!
NOW IN YOUR MIND SING IT TO THE TUNE OF *HAPPY BIRTHDAY*!
I'M A L-O-S-E-R I'M A L-O-S-E-R
WHAT HAPPENED?
IT JUST SEEMS LIKE WORDS IN A SONG AND DOESN'T BOTHER ME!

EXERCISE

Pick a thought that bothers you, and silently sing it to the tune 'Happy Birthday'.

What happens when you do that?

Notice that you haven't tried to challenge it, avoid it, or get rid of it. But hopefully you can now see it for what it is: nothing more or less than a string of words.

The mind LOVES its STORIES! Unfortunately many of these stories are UNHELPFUL.

I CAN'T COPE.
I'M NOT GOOD ENOUGH.
I HATE MY THIGHS.
THERE'S NO HOPE FOR THE FUTURE.

It's 'normal' for about 80 per cent of our thoughts to have some negative content. The trouble arises only when we FUSE with these thoughts and when we let them DOMINATE us. This feeds:

INSECURITY ANXIETY DEPRESSION
ANGER LOW SELF-ESTEEM SELF-DOUBT

Some psychological approaches advise you to:

- check the FACTS and correct MENTAL ERRORS
- make the story more POSITIVE
- tell yourself a better STORY
- DISTRACT yourself
- PUSH the story away
- DEBATE the truth of the story.

LA
LA
LA LA

But these strategies rarely work in the long run.

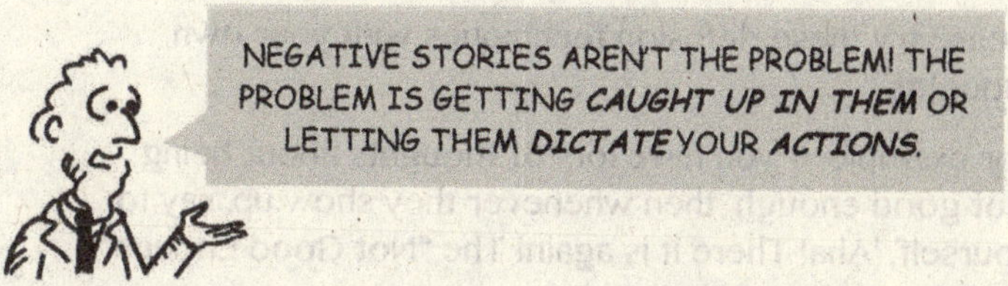
NEGATIVE STORIES AREN'T THE PROBLEM! THE PROBLEM IS GETTING *CAUGHT UP IN THEM* OR LETTING THEM *DICTATE* YOUR *ACTIONS*.

Just like those tabloid stories — you can BUY INTO them...

THAT'S *AWFUL*!
STAR DIES... OF EMBARRASSMENT
...or NOT!
BLIMEY! WHAT WILL THEY *DREAM UP* NEXT?

Trying to CHANGE, AVOID or GET RID OF a story is often INEFFECTIVE. Instead, simply name it for what it IS!

THIS IS A *STORY*!

Try naming your own stories and see they are nothing more than WORDS.

THE 'I'M A LOSER' STORY
THE 'I'M FAT' STORY
THE 'I CAN'T COPE' STORY
THE 'I'M UNLOVABLE' STORY

Please try these defusion techniques with your own thoughts.

For example, if you have lots of thoughts about being 'not good enough' then whenever they show up, say to yourself, 'Aha! There it is again! The "Not Good Enough" story.'

If you like, you can also add, with a sense of humour, 'Thanks, mind!'

WELL THAT'S ALL WELL AND GOOD BUT WHAT IF THE STORIES ARE *TRUE*?
I'M ALL ALONE!
GOOD POINT! WE'LL EXPLORE THAT NEXT!

Chapter 5

True blues

ACT: WHAT'S IMPORTANT IS NOT
WHETHER OR NOT A THOUGHT IS TRUE
BUT
WHETHER OR NOT IT HELPS YOU
TO HOLD ONTO IT!

EXAMPLE 1

UNHELPFUL

I'M INCOMPETENT!

Belittling/ Unsettling

Does holding onto that thought when it appears IMPROVE your performance?

HELPFUL

I COULD ASK FOR HELP.
IT. DEP

Expanding skills and knowledge

EXAMPLE 2

UNHELPFUL

I'M A LUMP OF LARD!

Blaming, demoralising

Does holding onto that thought when it appears make you want to LOOK AFTER yourself?

HELPFUL

I'LL GO FOR A WALK!

Making healthier choices!

EVEN IF IT'S *TRUE*!

BUT I REALLY *HAVE* BLOWN ALL MY SAVINGS!

Does getting caught in these thoughts help you COPE?

NO, I JUST FEEL MORE DEPRESSED AND THINK *WORSE* THOUGHTS!
PATHETIC!
LOSER!

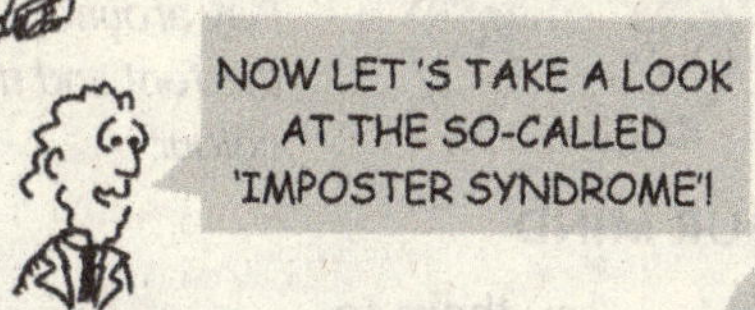
NOW LET 'S TAKE A LOOK AT THE SO-CALLED 'IMPOSTER SYNDROME'!

John does his job well. He's EFFICIENT and COMPETENT.

But his mind has OTHER IDEAS!

I'M A *FRAUD*. I'M JUST *LUCKY* THAT IT WORKED OUT. I'M SURE TO *BLOW IT* AND BE FOUND OUT!

With the IMPOSTER SYNDROME, John is paying more attention to his overcritical thoughts...

...than the direct experience

YOU DON'T KNOW WHAT YOU'RE DOING!
YOU'RE SCREWING IT UP!
YEAH, *RIGHT*!
THAT'S *PERFECT* JOHN!
THANKS.

John has been 'hooked' by the 'I'm Incompetent' story. He needs to 'unhook' himself and turn his attention to what's REALLY happening.

EXERCISES

1. NOT TAKING A THOUGHT SERIOUSLY

Imagine the thought on a computer screen.

Play around with the font and the colour.

2. THANKING YOUR MIND

When the same old stories come up,

MY LIFE'S *HOPELESS.*

say them to yourself with a sense of humour!

IS THAT *RIGHT?* THANKS FOR SHARING!
AHA! HERE IT IS AGAIN! THE '*MY LIFE'S HOPELESS* STORY!

OR simply —

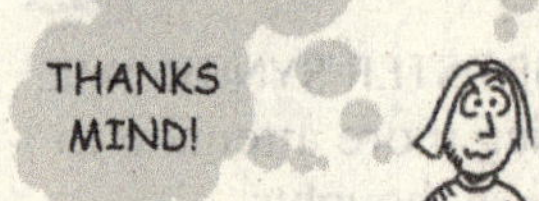
THANKS MIND!

3. SILLY VOICES

Pick a recurring self-judgement.

I'M STUPID!

Silently say it to yourself in the voice of a cartoon or movie character.

I'M STHTOOPID!

4. KIDS COMIC BOOK

I CAN'T DO IT!

Imagine your thought inside a thought bubble in a comic book.

SUPAGUY
I CAN'T DO IT!

Again, notice that you have not tried to avoid or change the thought, you've just seen it for what it is – WORDS.

BUT I HAVE *TERMINAL CANCER*! IF I HAVE A THOUGHT THAT I'LL BE DEAD SOON, THAT'S BOTH *TRUE* AND *SERIOUS*!
YES, BUT IS IT *HELPFUL* TO GET ENTANGLED IN THOSE THOUGHTS? DO YOU WANT TO SPEND THE TIME YOU HAVE LEFT STUCK INSIDE YOUR THOUGHTS OR DOING THINGS THAT *MATTER*?
I'M SORRY BUT I CAN'T DO THE SILLY VOICES FOR THIS. IT'S TOO *PAINFUL*!

That's fine; pick another technique that works for you.

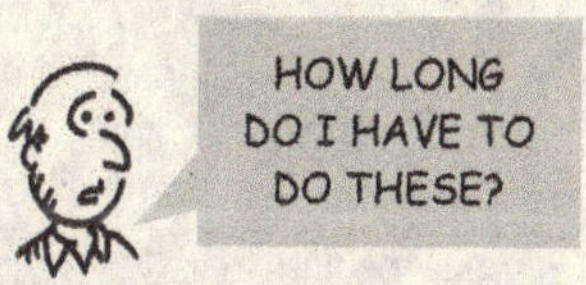
HOW LONG DO I HAVE TO DO THESE?

Until you are able to defuse your thoughts quickly.

DEFUSION GUIDELINES

- See the thoughts for what they are – nothing more or less than WORDS.
- Don't EXPECT anything. Just observe what happens.
- The thoughts may go or not. The technique may work sometimes but not at others.
- You're HUMAN – your thoughts will snare you again. But now you know how you can quickly unhook yourself.
- Like any skill, the more you practise the better you get.

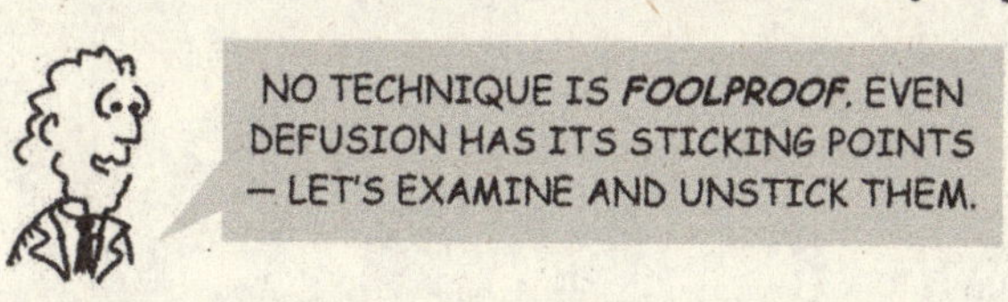
NO TECHNIQUE IS *FOOLPROOF*. EVEN DEFUSION HAS ITS STICKING POINTS – LET'S EXAMINE AND UNSTICK THEM.

Chapter 6

Troubleshooting defusion

I TRIED DEFUSION AND IT DOESN'T *WORK*.
YOU MEAN YOU STAYED *ENTANGLED* IN THE STORY?
NO. I UNHOOKED MYSELF BUT I STILL FELT *ANXIOUS*!
BUT DEFUSION IS NOT A WAY TO *CONTROL* YOUR FEELINGS!
THE PURPOSE OF DEFUSION IS...
...to see your thoughts as words and unhook yourself — so you can do the things that matter and engage in them fully.
BUT I DON'T *LIKE* FEELING ANXIOUS!
OF *COURSE*! NOBODY DOES!

But the more you struggle with painful feelings, the bigger they get! Later in the book we'll show you a new way to handle them!

HMPH! I DID THAT DEFUSION TECHNIQUE BUT THE THOUGHTS DIDN'T *GO AWAY*.
SOMETIMES THEY GO, SOMETIMES THEY STAY. WE'RE NOT TRYING TO GET RID OF THE THOUGHTS — JUST TO *UNHOOK* OURSELVES.
BUT SHOULDN'T I TRY TO THINK MORE *POSITIVELY*?
THE ISSUE IS NOT WHETHER YOUR THOUGHTS ARE *POSITIVE* OR *NEGATIVE*. THE QUESTION IS THIS...
IF I LET THIS THOUGHT GUIDE WHAT I DO, WILL IT HELP ME CREATE THE LIFE I WANT?
BUT POSITIVE THOUGHTS ARE ALWAYS *HELPFUL*, AREN'T THEY?

WELL, A DRUNK DRIVER MAY THINK HE'S COMPETENT TO DRIVE — THAT *IS* A POSITIVE THOUGHT, BUT IS IT *HELPFUL*?
CRASH!
BUT NEGATIVE THOUGHTS ARE *UNHELPFUL* RIGHT?

NOT NECESSARILY! IF A NEGATIVE THOUGHT LEADS TO *POSITIVE* ACTION, IT CAN BE *HELPFUL*.
I MIGHT SCREW UP THE TEST!
I'D BETTER GO DO SOME PREPARATION!

Negative thoughts are not the ENEMY! They are just WORDS and PICTURES floating through your mind. Fight them and you'll be fighting YOURSELF.

SO IS *FUSION* EVER *HELPFUL*?
IT CAN BE!

Planning your future, mentally rehearsing your actions, getting lost in a book can all be HELPFUL types of FUSION.

So when a thought appears, if it's helpful, USE it and if not, DEFUSE it.

Increase your AWARENESS of when and where you fuse, and the sorts of thoughts you tend to fuse with. The aim is to get better at catching yourself doing it, so you can then consciously choose how to act on those thoughts.

And like learning any new skill you'll need to PRACTISE till it becomes more natural to you. Pick ONE or TWO defusion techniques and practise them at every opportunity. AT LEAST 10 times a day but the more the better!

So if at this point your mind says:

IDIOT!
THEN DEFUSE!

STUPID THING TO SAY!
THEN DEFUSE!

MY LIFE SUCKS!
THEN DEFUSE!

And if you're now thinking...

IT'S ALL TOO HARD. I CAN'T BE BOTHERED.
DEFUSE FROM THAT TOO!

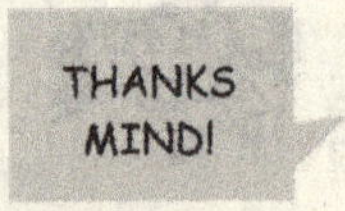
THANKS MIND!

There are TWO PARTS to your MIND:

THE THINKING SELF

is responsible for:

THINKING
PLANNING
JUDGING
COMPARING
CREATING
VISUALISING
IMAGINING
ANALYSING

THE OBSERVING SELF

is responsible for:

ATTENTION
AWARENESS
CONSCIOUSNESS
NOTICING
OBSERVING

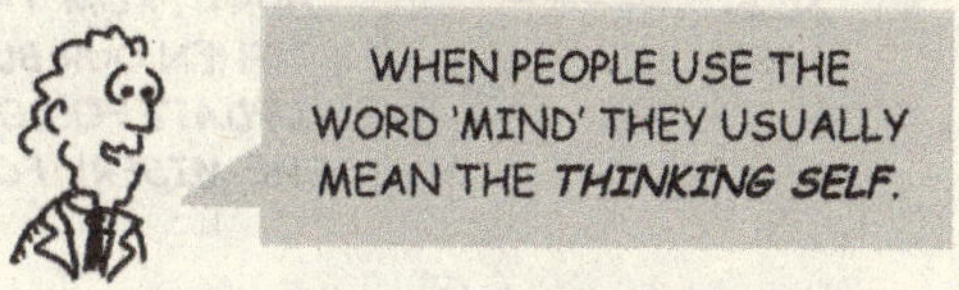

Life is like a STAGE SHOW and on that stage are all your THOUGHTS and FEELINGS and everything you can SEE, HEAR, TOUCH, TASTE and SMELL.

The OBSERVING SELF is the part of you that can step back and watch the show.

The OBSERVING SELF can zoom in and take in the DETAILS or zoom out and take in the WHOLE SHOW – and the show CONTINUALLY CHANGES.

EXERCISE

For 60 SECONDS, close your eyes and notice what THOUGHTS appear...

The THINKING SELF creates the thoughts. The OBSERVING SELF notices the thoughts.

Remember – because of the way it evolved, our mind is a bit like RADIO DOOM AND GLOOM:

IT'S RADIO DOOM AND GLOOM!
FIRST LET'S RE-RUN *A HURT FROM THE PAST*, THEN OUR *BUMMER UPDATE* FOLLOWED BY THE *MISERY FORECAST*!

And you can't turn it off! In fact, the HARDER you try, the LOUDER it gets!

EVEN MORE DOOM & GLOOM!
SHUT UP! SHUT UP! SHUT UP!

So if it's broadcasting a HELPFUL story, tune in, and let it guide your actions.

But if it's broadcasting something unhelpful, just let it chatter away in the BACKGROUND.

This doesn't mean you get into a debate with the radio...

LIFE SUCKS!
OH NO IT *DOESN'T*!

...or try to IGNORE it...

HEY! I'M *TALKIN'* TO YOU!
I CAN'T *HEAR* YOU!

...you just let it chatter away and ENGAGE in what you're doing.

> **EXERCISE**
>
> Take 10 SLOW, DEEP BREATHS. Focus fully on the BREATH and the sensations of BREATHING.
>
> 
>
> Now let your thoughts come and go like PASSING CARS. Acknowledge them but stay focused on your BREATHING.
>
> 
> HMM ... THERE GO MY *THOUGHTS*.
>
> If a thought SNAGS you, gently UNHOOK yourself and REFOCUS on your breathing.

BY PRACTISING THIS TECHNIQUE YOU LEARN HOW TO:

- let thoughts come and go
- recognise when you've become hooked on a thought
- unhook and refocus.

- Take what comes – let go of any expectations. If it relaxes you, great but that's a bonus, not the aim.
- It doesn't matter how often you get 'hooked'. Regular unhooking improves your skills.
- It's best to practise this for 5–10 minutes, two to three times a day.

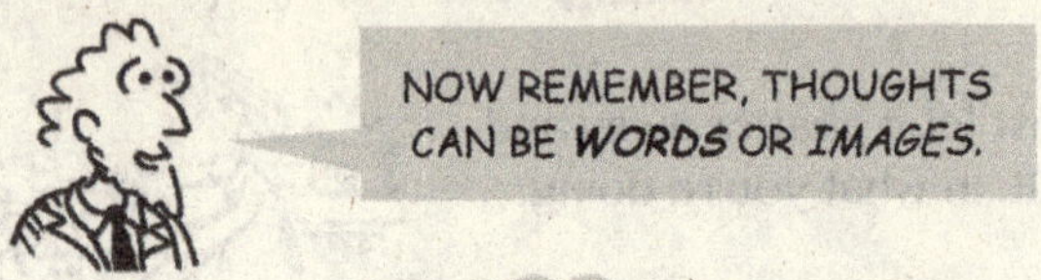
NOW REMEMBER, THOUGHTS CAN BE *WORDS* OR *IMAGES*.

We've all conjured up FRIGHTENING IMAGES in our heads...

NO WAY I'M GETTING ON *A PLANE*!

and fusing with these images can stop us doing what we VALUE.

When we FUSE with these images they seem very REAL or IMPORTANT or SCARY but we can DEFUSE from images, too. Try the following exercises:

EXERCISES

Bring to mind an unpleasant image. Notice how it affects you.

Imagine the image on a TV SCREEN.

Now play around with it – SLOW MOTION, BACKWARDS or change to BLACK AND WHITE.

ARF
ARF

FRA
FRA

See? It's just a PICTURE!

Now add a HUMOROUS TITLE or a SILLY VOICEOVER, or ODD MUSIC.

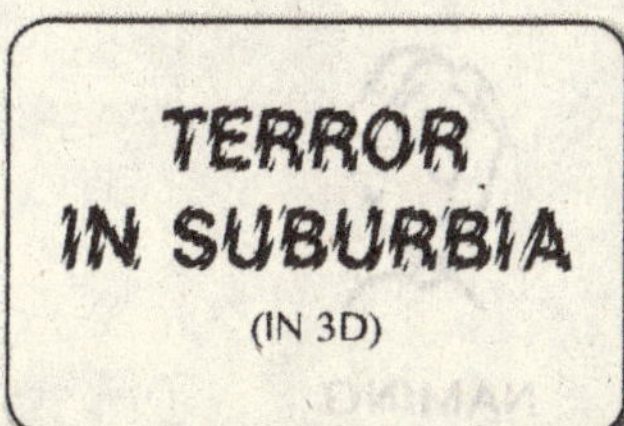
TERROR
IN SUBURBIA
(IN 3D)

And here in her natural habitat, we see Jenny...

DUM DUM DA DA!

(Tchaikovsky's 1812 overture)

Or try shifting the LOCATION of the troublesome image. Mentally picture it on a...

T SHIRT **CANVAS** **COMIC** **POSTAGE STAMP**

THE OLD HOME
HOME SWEET HOME

If the mental image is still pushing you around, run through these exercises every day till it loosens its grip. You can also adapt previous defusion techniques:

AHA! THE 'SCREWED IT UP' STORY!
I'M HAVING AN IMAGE OF...
I'M HAVING A MEMORY OF...

NAMING THE STORY **NAMING THE PICTURE**

or use...

THANKS MIND!

Here's one final technique (great for moving images).

Change your video clip...

ARF
ARF

...to a different GENRE!

CARTOON **WESTERN** **SCI-FI** **SOAP OPERA**

THE AIM IS TO *UNHOOK* — NOT TO GET RID OF THEM!
WHY?
BECAUSE THEY WILL COME BACK AGAIN AND AGAIN AND FIGHTING THEM IS *HARD WORK*!

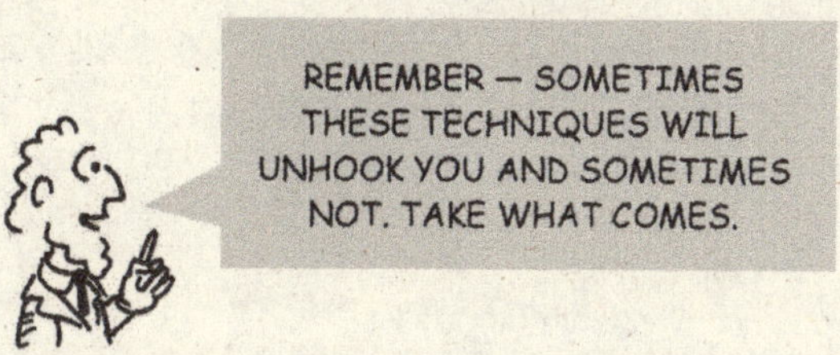
REMEMBER — SOMETIMES THESE TECHNIQUES WILL UNHOOK YOU AND SOMETIMES NOT. TAKE WHAT COMES.

Chapter 7

Demons in the boat

Imagine you are in a boat far out to SEA...

...and below deck are a bunch of demons which are EMOTIONS, THOUGHTS, FEELINGS and URGES.

GUILT
ADDICTION
SORROW
ANGER
SHAME

If you keep DRIFTING AIMLESSLY they stay below, but as you near land they clamber on deck and OVERWHELM you.

AARGH!

So you make a DEAL.

I'LL KEEP DRIFTING IF YOU STAY BELOW.
OKAY.

But drifting is not FUN.

ANXIOUS
BORED
LONELY
I *HATE* THIS!

Besides, other ships are happily landing. Why not YOURS?

But if you try to land, the demons will RESURFACE! WHAT TO DO?

You could try to throw the demons OVERBOARD...

...but then no-one would be steering and you might SINK.

And besides, there are TOO MANY to fight off.

But take a GOOD LOOK at those demons in BROAD DAYLIGHT and you'll discover that they're noisy and ugly but they can't actually HARM you.

GROWL!
GRUMP!

And once you get used to them they're not really THAT scary.

And you'll see they're much SMALLER than you thought!

They may never be cute and cuddly but they no longer have POWER over you.

YOU CAN'T CONTROL ME!

So now you can head to shore and do the things you LIKE!

Your demons love to pop up when you try new things but they can't STOP you!

Ask yourself:

- How would I act differently if my 'demons' were no longer a problem?
- What activities would I start (or continue)?
- What would I do, if fear wasn't a barrier?
- What would I stand for, if fear couldn't stop me?

(Are troublesome thoughts or images popping up for you? If so, you know how to defuse!)

Now let's explore the scariest demons of all – **PAINFUL EMOTIONS.**

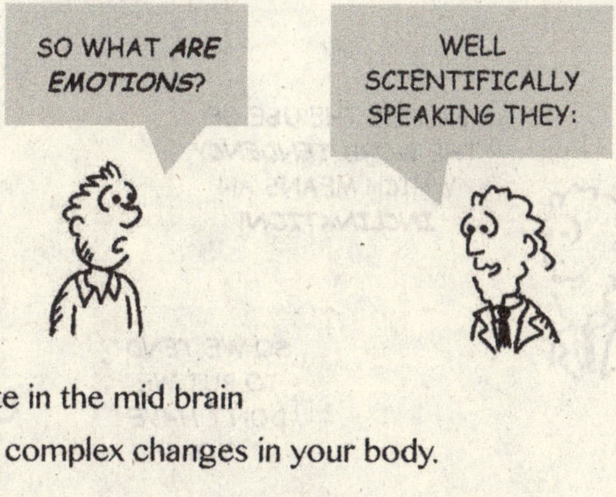
SO WHAT *ARE EMOTIONS*?
WELL SCIENTIFICALLY SPEAKING THEY:

- originate in the mid brain
- involve complex changes in your body.

These changes prepare us for action and lead to a TENDENCY to act in a certain way.

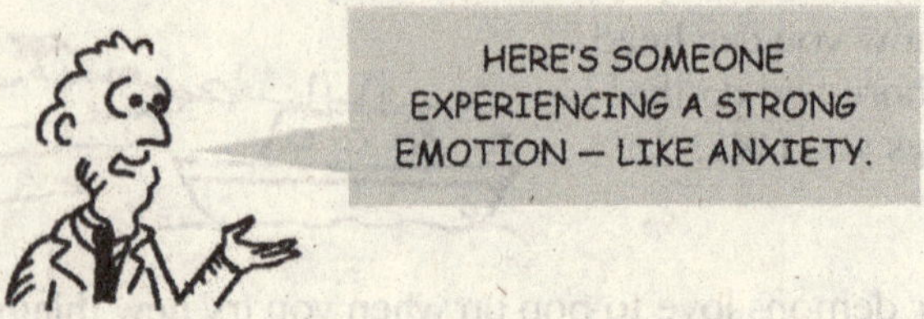
HERE'S SOMEONE
EXPERIENCING A STRONG
EMOTION — LIKE ANXIETY.

PHYSICAL SENSATIONS

Fast shallow breathing

Increased heart rate

Sweating

Churning stomach

Urge to run

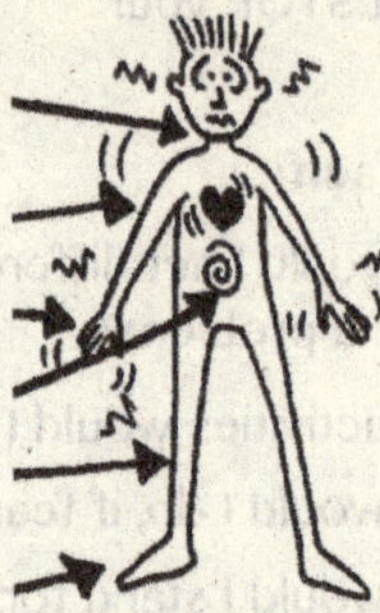

ACTION TENDENCY

Talk rapidly

Fidget

Pace up and down

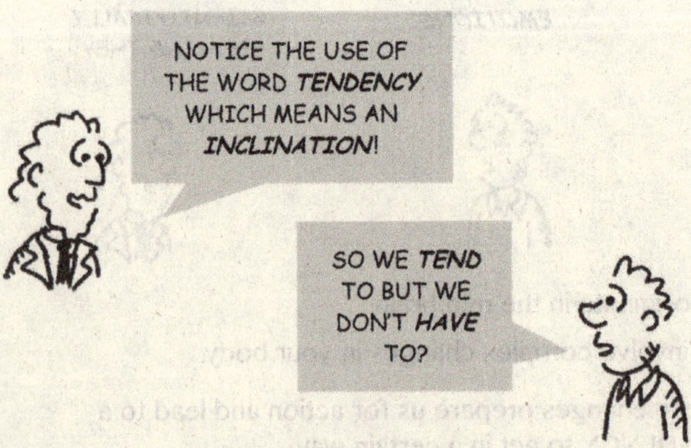
NOTICE THE USE OF
THE WORD *TENDENCY*
WHICH MEANS AN
INCLINATION!
SO WE *TEND*
TO BUT WE
DON'T *HAVE*
TO?

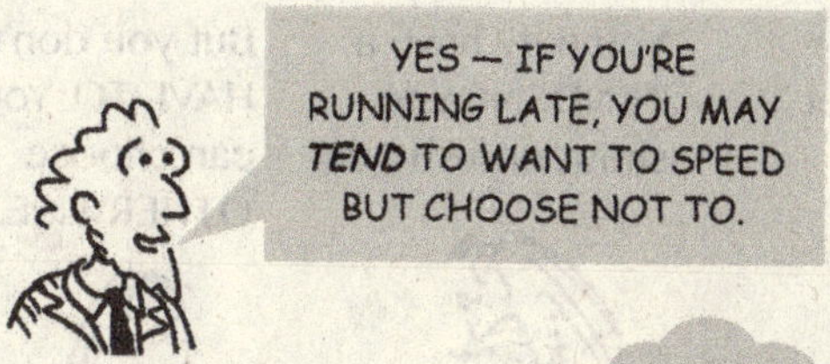
YES — IF YOU'RE RUNNING LATE, YOU MAY *TEND* TO WANT TO SPEED BUT CHOOSE NOT TO.

WHOA! TAKE IT *EASY*!

Emotions are made up of: WORDS and IMAGES in your head and SENSATIONS and FEELINGS in your body.

I'M SCARED THIS MIGHT GO WRONG.

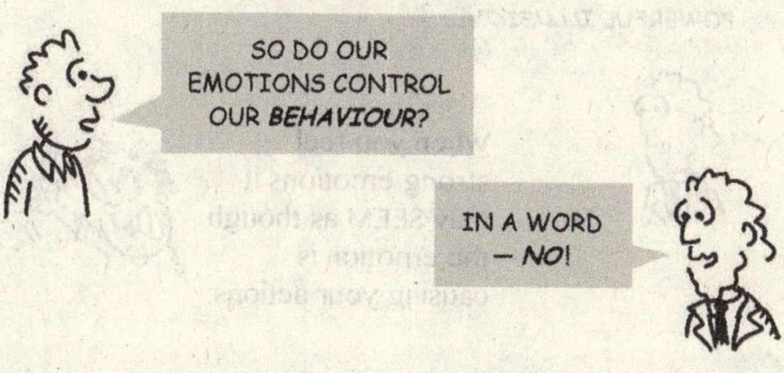
SO DO OUR EMOTIONS CONTROL OUR *BEHAVIOUR*?
IN A WORD — *NO*!

You can feel ANGRY but act CALM.

You may have a TENDENCY to shout or lash out.

But you don't HAVE TO. You can choose OTHERWISE.

You may have felt fear ... and a TENDENCY to run...

GULP!

...but you chose NOT TO.

But though you may not have direct control over your FEELINGS...

YIKES!

...you can directly control your ACTIONS.

DON'T RUN! BACK AWAY SLOWLY!
?

THE IDEA THAT EMOTIONS CONTROL ACTIONS IS A POWERFUL *ILLUSION*!

When you feel strong emotions it may SEEM as though the emotion is causing your actions.

But with practice, you can control how you act, even when feeling very strong emotions.

Even when you're FURIOUS you can still...

- stand still
- speak softly
- drink water
- go to the toilet.

Emotions are like the weather – ever changing and always present.

MILD **PLEASANT**

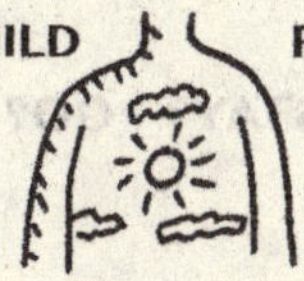

PREDICTABLE

INTENSE **UNPLEASANT**

UNEXPECTED

Some people are very in touch with and can express their feelings...

I FEEL ANXIOUS AND AGITATED.

...while others are more disconnected and have difficulty accessing their feelings.

I DUNNO, I FEEL OKAY I GUESS.

There are THREE PHASES in the creation of an emotion:

1 A significant event occurs either **INTERNALLY (e.g. a thought)**

I'M BAD.

or **EXTERNALLY**

and your brain registers this as IMPORTANT...

2 ...and does an EVALUATION

GOOD? BAD?

...and prepares you for APPROPRIATE ACTION.

STAY? GO?

3 The mind then tells a STORY about the experience...

FRUSTRATING?
JOYOUS?
SAD?
EXCITING?
GUILTY?

...which others may or may not SHARE.

THIS IS *FUN*!
THIS IS *AWFUL*!

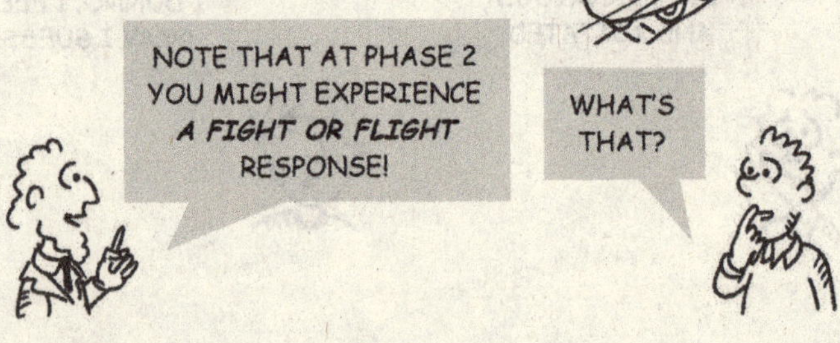
NOTE THAT AT PHASE 2 YOU MIGHT EXPERIENCE *A FIGHT OR FLIGHT* RESPONSE!
WHAT'S THAT?

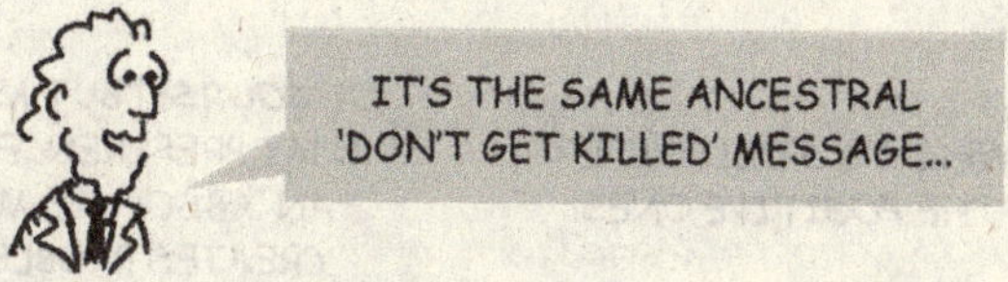
IT'S THE SAME ANCESTRAL
'DON'T GET KILLED' MESSAGE...

To save yourself you either stand and FIGHT the woolly mammoth...

...or take FLIGHT!

Our minds have evolved to look for danger EVERYWHERE...

A MOODY SPOUSE

A BIG MORTGAGE

A CONTROLLING BOSS

OR EVEN A FRIGHTENING THOUGHT!

The fight or flight response triggers unpleasant or 'negative' feelings.

GUILT

FEAR

However, if our brain registers the event as 'good' then pleasant 'positive' feelings are triggered.

JOY

PLEASURE

DELIGHT

But 'NEGATIVE' and 'POSITIVE' are just LABELS for what are simply FEELINGS.

WELL I'D STILL PREFER THE *POSITIVE* ONES!
OF *COURSE*! BUT MAKING THAT PREFERENCE INTO AN 'ABSOLUTE MUST' CREATES PROBLEMS.
SO LET'S LOOK AT A NEW WAY TO HANDLE PAINFUL FEELINGS.

Chapter 8

Drop the struggle

Most of us readily buy into STORIES about painful emotions such as:

ANGER GUILT SHAME FEAR EMBARRASSMENT AND ANXIETY ARE 'NEGATIVE' EMOTIONS.
WHICH ARE *BAD* *DANGEROUS* *IRRATIONAL* AND A SIGN OF *WEAKNESS*.
AND SHOW *I HAVE PSYCHOLOGICAL DEFECTS*.
THEY'LL DAMAGE MY *HEALTH*.
PEOPLE SHOULD *HIDE* THEIR FEELINGS.
THEY SHOW A LACK OF *CONTROL*.
I MUST KEEP MY EMOTIONS UNDER *CONTROL*.
WOMEN SHOULDN'T GET *ANGRY*.
MEN SHOULDN'T FEEL *AFRAID*.

IF I DON'T CONTROL MY FEELINGS SOMETHING *BAD* WILL HAPPEN!
NEGATIVE EMOTION MEANS THERE'S SOMETHING *WRONG* WITH MY LIFE.

Your outlook on expressing emotion is heavily influenced by your CHILDHOOD PROGRAMMING. Negative emotions may have been...

SUPPRESSED

CHEER UP! ITS ONLY *A DOLL*!
FOR GOODNESS SAKE 'BE *A MAN*'!

IF ALLOWED, COULD HAVE BEEN FRIGHTENING

GET IT OFF YOUR *CHEST*!

EXERCISE

Take note of your childhood programming about EMOTIONS.

1. What messages were you given?
2. Which emotions were you told were desirable or undesirable?
3. What were you told about the best way to handle emotions?
4. What emotions did your family freely express? Suppress? Frown upon? Hide?
5. With which emotions were your family comfortable? Uncomfortable?
6. How did the adults handle their own emotions?
7. How did they react to your emotions?
8. What did you learn from observing this as you grew?
9. What ideas do you still retain from your programming?

JUDGING OUR EMOTIONS

We tend to judge emotions according to how they FEEL.

ACT – let go of judging and see them as what they are:

Constantly changing SENSATIONS moving through your body.

- **No emotion is 'GOOD' or 'BAD'.**
- **An emotion may be PAINFUL or PLEASANT but if we FUSE with the thought that it's BAD, we will struggle with it and make it WORSE.**

MY FAMILY DIDN'T OPENLY EXPRESS LOVE AND AFFECTION. I FEEL *UNCOMFORTABLE* DOING SO.
BUT DOES THAT MAKE THESE FEELINGS *BAD?*
WELL I *HATE* FEELING ANXIOUS!
OF *COURSE*! IT'S UNPLEASANT! *NO-ONE* ENJOYS IT!

Your mind WILL judge your feelings but you can DEFUSE from these judgements. Here are some examples of DEFUSION TECHNIQUES you can use:

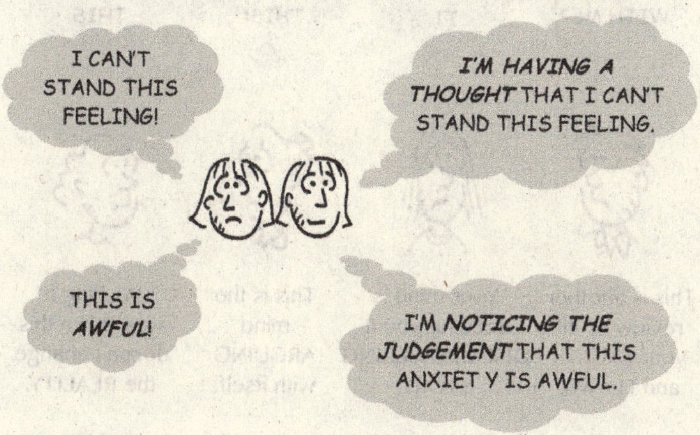
I CAN'T STAND THIS FEELING!
I'M HAVING A THOUGHT THAT I CAN'T STAND THIS FEELING.
THIS IS *AWFUL!*
I'M *NOTICING THE JUDGEMENT* THAT THIS ANXIET Y IS AWFUL.

Judging ADDS to emotional discomfort and so does...

REVIEWING

WHY AM I FEELING LIKE THIS?

Reviewing all your PROBLEMS creates the illusion that your life is nothing BUT problems.

REHASHING

WHAT HAVE I DONE TO DESERVE THIS?

Rehashing all your 'CRIMES' to explain this 'PUNISHMENT' leads to SELF-BLAME.

SEARCHING

WHY AM I LIKE THIS?

Searching your life history for someone to BLAME can lead to anger, resentment and hopelessness.

WHAT'S WRONG WITH ME?

This is another review of all your FAULTS and FLAWS.

I CAN'T HANDLE IT.

Your mind is feeding you a DISEMPOWERING STORY.

I SHOULDN'T FEEL LIKE THIS!

This is the mind ARGUING with itself.

I WISH I DIDN'T FEEL LIKE THIS.

Wishing it wasn't like this doesn't change the REALITY.

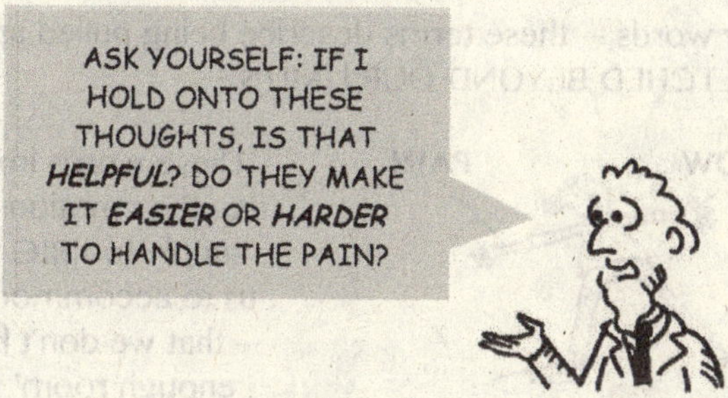
ASK YOURSELF: IF I HOLD ONTO THESE THOUGHTS, IS THAT *HELPFUL*? DO THEY MAKE IT *EASIER* OR *HARDER* TO HANDLE THE PAIN?

When we feel painful feelings we naturally do what we can to AVOID or GET RID OF them.

But often the things that give us RELIEF in the SHORT TERM...

...make our life WORSE in the LONG TERM.

SO HOW DO WE *COPE* WITH PAINFUL FEELINGS?
WE LEARN A SKILL CALLED 'EXPANSION'.

In order to understand EXPANSION look at some words that describe FEELING BAD:

TENSION – being stretched or stressed

STRESS – subject to strain or pressure

STRAIN – to shock beyond proper limits.

In other words – these terms describe being pulled apart or STRETCHED BEYOND OUR LIMITS.

SORROW
PAIN
GUILT
GRIEF

These words imply that the emotions are simply too BIG for us to accommodate – that we don't have 'enough room' for them.

NOW LET'S LOOK AT WHAT WE MEAN BY *EXPANSION*:

EXPAND: spread unfold develop.

BUT IF I OPEN UP TO MY FEELINGS THEY'LL TAKE OVER AND I'LL *LOSE CONTROL*!
THAT'S JUST YOUR MIND TELLING YOU *SCARY STORIES*! THANK IT AND MAKE ROOM FOR OTHER POSSIBILITIES.

BEFORE WE GO ANY FURTHER, LET'S REVISIT A VERY HELPFUL IDEA.
OH? WHAT IS IT?

REMEMBER THE TWO PARTS TO YOUR MIND, THE THINKING SELF AND OBSERVING SELF?
AH YES! CAN YOU REMIND ME AGAIN?
CERTAINLY...

The **THINKING SELF** is

THOUGHTS
MOVEMENTS
IMAGES
MEMORIES

The **OBSERVING SELF** is

AWARENESS
ATTENTION
FOCUS

EXERCISE

Use your OBSERVING SELF to notice what is happening in your body and let your THOUGHTS come and go like a radio in the background.

Is your BREATHING SHALLOW? DEEP? FAST? SLOW?

How does your MOUTH feel? WARM? COOL? WET? DRY?

Position of ARMS?

Is there any tension in your NECK or SHOULDERS?

Do you feel HOT or COLD? WHERE do you feel this?

Is your SPINE STRAIGHT or BENT?

Position of LEGS?

How are your FEET placed?

Scan your whole body and notice any TENSION, PAIN or DISCOMFORT.

Now notice any PLEASANT or COMFORTABLE sensations.

Do you feel like SHIFTING? Shift and notice how it feels.

Do you feel any urge to EAT, SLEEP, SCRATCH, STRETCH?

NOTICING your body is different to THINKING about it.

THINKING SELF gives the 'commentary'.

WHAT'S THE *POINT* OF THIS?
I HOPE I'M DOING IT *RIGHT*.

OBSERVING SELF just notices the sensations.

And sometimes, for brief moments when you are observing the THINKING SELF shuts up!

In EXPANSION we sidestep our thoughts and connect with our emotions through the OBSERVING SELF. In doing so, we experience emotions as they are rather than as the THINKING SELF says they are i.e. we NOTICE rather than THINK.

BUT MY THOUGHTS *NEVER SHUT UP*!
YES YOUR THINKING SELF WILL TRY TO *DISTRACT* YOU...
THIS FEELS *BAD.*
I'M *SCARED*
I CAN'T *HANDLE* THIS.
IT'S TOO *HARD.*
I'LL DO THIS *LATER.*
SO WHAT DO I *DO*?
JUST LET THE THOUGHTS GO BY LIKE *PASSING CARS.*

When there is traffic outside your window you don't leap up to check every car! Likewise, you don't have to respond to every THOUGHT!

But if a 'screeching tyre' distracts you, simply REFOCUS.

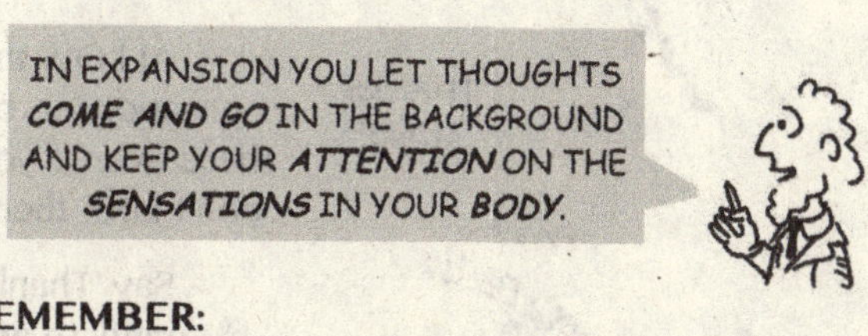
IN EXPANSION YOU LET THOUGHTS *COME AND GO* IN THE BACKGROUND AND KEEP YOUR *ATTENTION* ON THE *SENSATIONS* IN YOUR *BODY.*

REMEMBER:

- ▶ Emotions arise from PHYSICAL CHANGES in the body.
- ▶ Focus on their PHYSICAL SENSATIONS.

EXPANSION WITH PAINFUL EMOTIONS: 3 steps

1 OBSERVE Scan your body for uncomfortable feelings.

Are they STILL or MOVING?

How DEEP do they go?

Where are they STRONGEST? WEAKEST?

Where do they START and END?

Find the sensation that bothers you most and observe it with CURIOSITY and OPENNESS.

2 BREATHE

SLOW, DEEP BREATHS

Breathe directly INTO and AROUND sensations and make ROOM for them.

It's as if you open up and expand AROUND the feelings.

3 ALLOW

THANKS MIND!
EEK!!

ALLOW the sensations to be there even if you don't LIKE them.

Say 'Thanks mind' to any RESISTANCE.

Simply acknowledge any unhelpful thoughts.

Don't try to GET RID OF the sensation or ALTER it. The goal is to see it as it is, and make PEACE with it. Focus on the sensation until you DROP THE STRUGGLE WITH IT. Then move onto another sensation until you are no longer fighting them.

NOW BRING TO MIND SOMETHING THAT *DISTRESSES* YOU.
ARE YOU *CRAZY?* I DON'T WANT TO FEEL THAT DISCOMFORT!
YOU MAY NOT *WANT* TO BUT CAN YOU BE *WILLING* TO?
WHY *SHOULD* I?
BECAUSE THROUGHOUT YOUR LIFE UNCOMFORTABLE FEELINGS *WILL* ARISE.
AND TRYING TO AVOID THEM OFTEN JUST CREATES MORE PROBLEMS.

By being WILLING to feel them they'll have less impact and influence over you.

BUT ISN'T THAT *MASOCHISTIC*?
ONLY IF IT SERVES NO *GOOD PURPOSE*!
SO WHAT'S THE *GOOD PURPOSE*?
IMPROVING YOUR *HEALTH* AND TO LEARN VALUABLE SKILLS TO *TRANSFORM YOUR LIFE*!
OKAY, I'LL *GIVE IT A GO*!
GOOD! SO BRING TO MIND SOMETHING THAT *DISTRESSES* YOU, GET IN TOUCH WITH *A PAINFUL FEELING*, AND PRACTISE THE 3 STEPS OF EXPANSION.

EXERCISE

Please practise the 3-step exercise described above, for 3 to 5 minutes, two or three times a day.

In the next chapter, we'll look at any difficulties you may encounter.

Chapter 9

Troubleshooting expansion

The concept of EXPANSION is simple but it's not EASY! But like any meaningful challenge it's worth the effort. Let's explore some of the difficulties you may encounter in the beginning and troubleshoot them.

I TRIED MAKING ROOM FOR THE FEELINGS BUT THEY WERE TOO OVERWHELMING!
DON'T TRY TO TAKE ON TOO MUCH. JUST DO ONE SENSATION FIRST THEN THE NEXT.
WOW! THE FEELINGS DISAPPEARED!
ENJOY THAT WHEN IT HAPPENS — BUT REMEMBER, IT'S A BONUS, NOT THE MAIN AIM.
I MADE ROOM BUT THE FEELINGS WERE STILL THERE!
THEY WILL COME AND STAY AND GO IN THEIR OWN GOOD TIME.

OKAY, I'VE MADE ROOM FOR MY FEELINGS, *NOW WHAT?*
NOW IT'S TIME TO TAKE EFFECTIVE ACTION IN LINE WITH YOUR *VALUES*.
WHY DO YOU KEEP COMING BACK TO *ACTION* AND *VALUES?*
TO CREATE A *RICH* AND *FULL* LIFE WE NEED TO ACT ON OUR VALUES (AS YOU'LL SEE LATER IN THIS BOOK).
IS SLOW, DEEP BREATHING ESSENTIAL?
NO, BUT IT'S HELPFUL. *OBSERVING* AND *ALLOWING* ARE KEY, THOUGH.
BUT WHEN I'M UPSET I JUST GO *NUMB*!
MAKE *ROOM* FOR YOUR NUMBNESS FIRST. YOU MAY FIND OTHER FEELINGS FOLLOW.

HOW CAN I DO THIS EXERCISE IF I'M AT WORK OR SOMEWHERE *PUBLIC*?
DO IT *QUICKLY*! TAKE A DEEP BREATH AND MAKE ROOM FOR THE FEELING. THEN ENGAGE IN THE TASK AT HAND.
CAN THE *THINKING* SELF HELP EXPANSION?
YES — WITH *SELF-TALK* AND *IMAGERY*.

EXPANSION SELF-TALK

I DON'T *LIKE* THIS FEELING BUT I HAVE *ROOM* FOR IT.
IT'S UNPLEASANT BUT I *ACCEPT* IT.
I'M HAVING THE *FEELING* OF...
I DON'T *LIKE* IT OR *WANT* IT BUT I WON'T *FIGHT* IT.

EXPANSION IMAGERY

Scan for unpleasant feelings. Visualise the sensation as an object.

What size?
Shape?
Colour?
Texture?
Fixed?
Shifting?

Now breathe into it and make room for it.

HOW MUCH PRACTICE DO I NEED TO DO?
AT LEAST 3 TIMES A DAY, BUT THE MORE THE BETTER! TRAINING MAKES YOU SKILFUL.

BUT ISN'T IT UNHEALTHY TO KEEP FOCUSING ON UNPLEASANT FEELINGS?
YES, IF YOU ARE CONSTANTLY DWELLING ON THEM BUT NOT IF YOU ARE LEARNING EXPANSION SKILLS.

The aim is to let your feelings come and stay and go without a STRUGGLE. Focus on them ONLY to practise expansion. Otherwise, focus on doing what you VALUE.

Chapter 10

Great connections

HELLO?
ANYONE
HOME?

We've all 'drifted off' at times.

The **THINKING SELF** has one job only: to generate thoughts. But sometimes these thoughts can be DISTRACTING.

This is how we habitually go through most of our lives!

I DON'T REMEMBER HALF THE JOURNEY!

How much do you give your FULL ATTENTION to:

EATING?

WORKING?

I MUST HAVE READ THIS PAGE *SIX TIMES*!

READING?

There are times when being absorbed in our thoughts ASSISTS what we are doing...

HMM, HOW CAN I *SOLVE* THIS?

But too often it DOESN'T.

I'VE GOT NOTHING TO SAY! HE THINKS I'M *BORING*!
MUST DO MY TAXES!

We become DISCONNECTED. This is where CONNECTION comes in.

WHAT'S THAT?

IT'S BEING FULLY PRESENT AND AWAKE IN THE *HERE* AND *NOW* AND BEING CURIOUS ABOUT AND OPEN TO WHATEVER IS HAPPENING.

WHY IS THIS *IMPORTANT*?
SO YOU CAN ENGAGE *FULLY* IN LIFE.
TO FULLY APPRECIATE YOUR LIFE YOU NEED TO GIVE IT YOUR ATTENTION!
YOU COULD BE EATING THE MOST BEAUTIFUL MEAL OF YOUR LIFE BUT IF YOU'RE LOST IN YOUR THOUGHTS YOU'LL HARDLY EVEN *TASTE* IT.
PRESENT
PAST
FUTURE
WORK WAS *HELL* TODAY.
I HOPE I DON'T LOOK *GREEDY*!
WILL I GET THAT REPORT IN ON *TIME*?

As LEO TOLSTOY put it...

THERE IS ONLY ONE TIME THAT IS IMPORTANT: **NOW!**

We can only ever take action here and now, and to take effective and valuable action we need to be fully present.

CONNECTION is:

- waking up
- noticing what's happening
- appreciating the fullness of every moment.

This comes NATURALLY in life's wonderful moments, but it's hard to do when life is DIFFICULT or PAINFUL!

Here's a comparison between **FUSION** and **CONNECTION**:

FUSION	**CONNECTION**	**FUSION**	**CONNECTION**
DISTRACTED	ENGAGED	JUDGEMENTAL	DEFUSED FROM JUDGEMENTS

WHAT'S OVER *THERE?*

This should be better
I shouldn't be like this
THIS IS WRONG!

FUSION

EASILY BORED, KNOWS IT ALL

BEEN THERE, DONE THAT!

CONNECTION

CURIOUS & PRESENT

FUSION

LIVES IN PAST OR FUTURE

IF ONLY
WHAT IF?

FUSION

CLOSED OFF

THIS SUCKS!

CONNECTION

OPEN

THINKING SELF

STRUGGLES AGAINST REALITY

THIS CAN'T BE HAPPENING!

OBSERVING SELF

NOTICES & OPENS TO REALITY

OKAY I'M *GAME*. WHAT DO I DO?
TRY THESE EXERCISES.

CONNECTION EXERCISES

GUIDELINES

If thoughts or feelings distract you:

- let them come and go
- bring back your attention when it wanders (and it will!)
- silently say 'Thanks Mind'.

1. Connection with ENVIRONMENT — 30 seconds

Put the book down and notice your SURROUNDINGS.

Use all your senses. Notice five things that you can:
HEAR
SEE
FEEL.

2. Awareness of your BODY — 30 seconds

Notice the POSITION of your whole BODY.

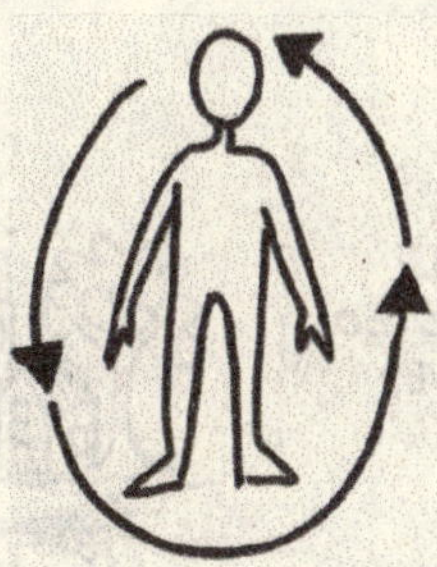

Do an internal scan and notice what you feel in EVERY PART.

3. Awareness of BREATH — 30 seconds

Connect with your BREATHING.

Notice the FLOW in and out. Notice what your body does with the breath.

4. Awareness of SOUNDS — 30 seconds

HUMMM
RRR

What do you HEAR?

SO, WHAT DID YOU NOTICE?
I DIDN'T REALISE THERE WAS SO MUCH GOING ON THAT I'D *MISSED*!
WE ARE SO EASILY *DISCONNECTED* AREN'T WE?

When we fuse with the stories our mind tells us, it keeps us DISCONNECTED from all that life offers.

I'M SINGLE AND LONELY AND NOW I'M EVEN OLDER!
HAPPY BIRTHDAY, JANE!

The more we get caught up in unpleasant THOUGHTS and FEELINGS, the more we are cut off from what's ACTUALLY happening and our chance to engage with what we DO want.

NOBODY WILL LOVE ME!
WE LOVE YOU, JANE!

We can get hooked by DOOM and GLOOM about the FUTURE:

IT MIGHT
BE *AWFUL*!

We can get hooked by DOOM and GLOOM about the PAST:

I LOST
EVERYTHING!

THERE'S
NO POINT!

It's hard to enjoy what you're doing if you're not connected with it, if you're LOST IN THOUGHTS!

But the REVERSE is also true!

I'M
REALLY
INTO
THIS!

So CONNECTION is an important skill for getting the MOST out of life.

EXERCISE: CONNECT WITH PLEASANT ACTIVITIES

Practise connection with at least one pleasant activity each day.

EXERCISE: CONNECTION WITH A USEFUL CHORE

Pick a chore you don't like and practise connection.

- Have no EXPECTATIONS.
- Just NOTICE what you do.
- Open your SENSES to what's happening.
- If you feel boredom or frustration MAKE ROOM for it.
- If your attention wanders, thank your mind and REFOCUS.

EXERCISE: CONNECTION WITH A TASK YOU'VE BEEN AVOIDING

Pick a task you've been putting off.

Set aside 20 minutes and make a start on it with connection.

After 20 minutes you are free to stop or continue.

Do 20 minutes a day
till the task is completed.

Practising connection is like building MUSCLES to strengthen your ability to handle change and move on with your life.

And important changes usually involve DISCOMFORT.

NEW CAREER ➡ Starting from scratch

ASKING SOMEONE OUT ➡ Possible rejection

AVOIDANCE = NO CHANGE/STUCK

CONNECTION = MOVEMENT/IMPROVEMENT

AREN'T THE REWARDS *WORTH IT?*

You can CONNECT, DEFUSE and EXPAND... or NOT! The choice is yours.

Another word that describes a process of DEFUSION, EXPANSION and CONNECTION is 'MINDFULNESS'.

This is not about having a 'FULL MIND'!

The *ACT* definition of MINDFULNESS would be:

- paying attention with openness and curiosity
- making room for whatever thoughts and feelings arise
- engaging fully in your here-and-now experience.

EXERCISE: MINDFUL BREATHING

Take six slow deep breaths. After a full out breath, breathe in gently. (If you're doing it right, your tummy will expand.) Practise connection: notice your breath flowing in and out!

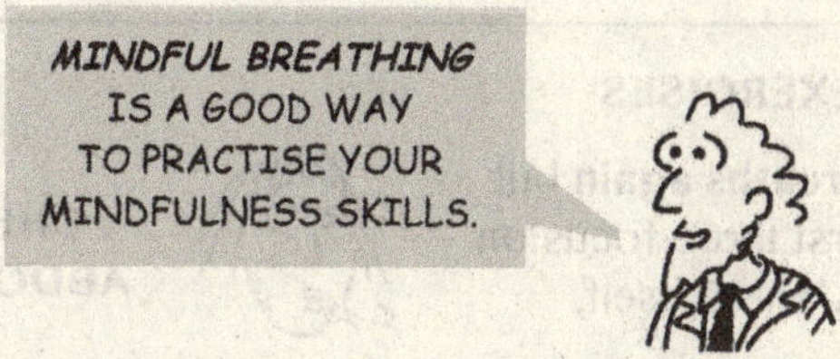
MINDFUL BREATHING IS A GOOD WAY TO PRACTISE YOUR MINDFULNESS SKILLS.

What did you notice?

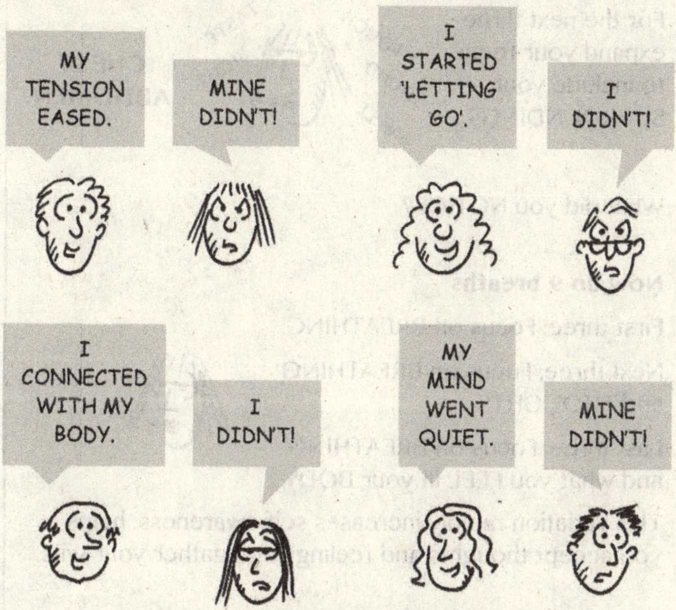
MY TENSION EASED.
MINE DIDN'T!
I STARTED 'LETTING GO'.
I DIDN'T!
I CONNECTED WITH MY BODY.
I DIDN'T!
MY MIND WENT QUIET.
MINE DIDN'T!

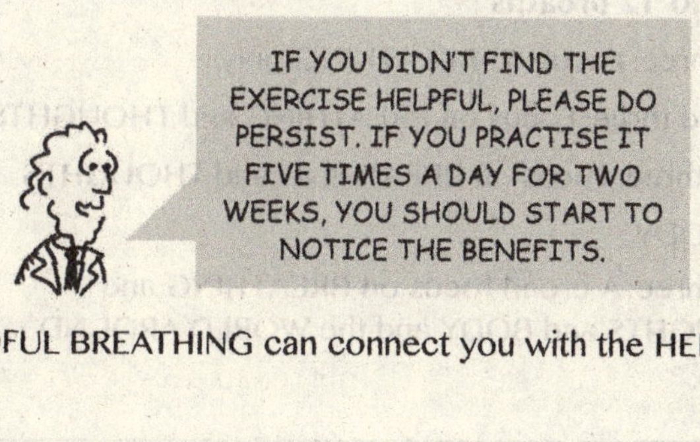
IF YOU DIDN'T FIND THE EXERCISE HELPFUL, PLEASE DO PERSIST. IF YOU PRACTISE IT FIVE TIMES A DAY FOR TWO WEEKS, YOU SHOULD START TO NOTICE THE BENEFITS.

MINDFUL BREATHING can connect you with the HERE and NOW.

THREE EXERCISES

Take 6 breaths again but for the first three focus on the BREATHING itself.

For the next three expand your focus to include your SURROUNDINGS.

What did you NOTICE?

Now do 9 breaths

First three: Focus on BREATHING.

Next three: Focus on BREATHING and THOUGHTS.

Last three: Focus on BREATHING and what you FEEL in your BODY.

This variation rapidly increases self-awareness, helps you accept thoughts and feelings and gather your wits.

Now do 12 breaths

First three: Focus on BREATHING only.

Second three: Focus on BREATHING and THOUGHTS.

Third three: Focus on BREATHING and THOUGHTS and BODY.

Final three: A broad focus on BREATHING and THOUGHTS and BODY and the WORLD AROUND YOU.

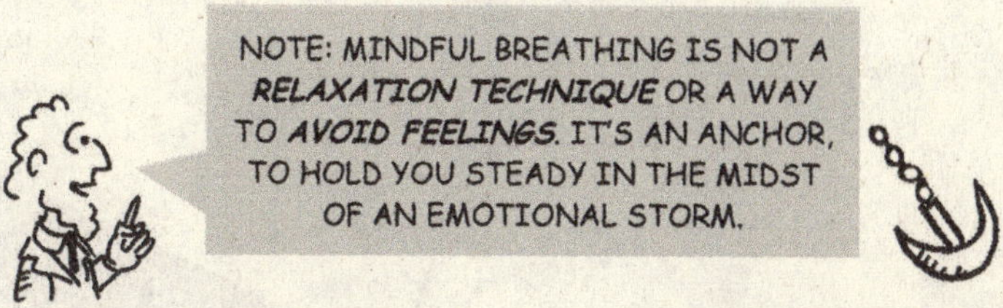
NOTE: MINDFUL BREATHING IS NOT A *RELAXATION TECHNIQUE* OR A WAY TO *AVOID FEELINGS*. IT'S AN ANCHOR, TO HOLD YOU STEADY IN THE MIDST OF AN EMOTIONAL STORM.

REMEMBER – EVEN ONE SLOW, DEEP BREATH CAN HELP TO ANCHOR YOU UNTIL THE STORM PASSES.

Fancy a CHALLENGE?

EXERCISE

(Allow 10 minutes, once or twice a day.)

Sit or lie comfortably.

Let your thoughts come and go.

Focus on your breath for 6 minutes.

When your attention wanders, refocus.

For the next 3 minutes focus attention on your body, and its feelings and sensations.

For the final minute open your eyes and take in the room around you.

Regular practice will bring noticeable PHYSICAL and PSYCHOLOGICAL benefits.

Chapter 11

You're not who you think you are

What do you most DISLIKE about yourself?

These are only a few of the most common responses. The range is infinite but there is one basic theme:

No matter how hard we try or what we achieve, our THINKING SELF always finds FAULT with us.

YOU MIGHT TELL YOURSELF GOOD THINGS ABOUT YOURSELF...
I'M DOING WELL AT MY JOB. I EAT WELL, EXERCISE, I'M GENEROUS. THEREFORE I'M A GOOD PERSON.
AND IF YOU CAN TRULY BELIEVE THAT YOU ARE A GOOD PERSON YOU WILL FEEL GOOD.
BUT ALL TOO OFTEN YOU FIND YOURSELF HAVING TO PROVE OR JUSTIFY THIS POSITION...
I'M GOOD...
...AREN'T I?
...OR HAVING TO DISPUTE THE 'NOT GOOD ENOUGH' STORIES THAT CREEP IN.

So like a game of chess, you find yourself constantly caught in a battle between 'GOOD' and 'BAD' thoughts and feelings.

I'M A NICE GUY.
I'M SELFISH.

You advance the 'Good Guys' across the board...

I JUST GOT A PROMOTION.
I HELPED MY FRIENDS.
I'M GOING TO THE GYM.

...only to find a whole army of 'Bad Guys' waiting to counterattack.

YOU BLEW THAT PRESENTATION!
YOU MISSED YOUR RUN ... YOU'RE LAZY!
YOUR FRIEND HASN'T CALLED YOU – HE HATES YOU!

Trying to feel good about yourself through positive AFFIRMATIONS will have LIMITED success...

I LOVE & APPROVE OF MYSELF!
I AM A WONDERFUL HUMAN BEING.

Firstly, you are unlikely to BELIEVE it any more than saying...

I'M SUPERMAN!
I'M WONDER WOMAN!

...secondly, even if what you're saying rings TRUE...

I'M A KIND AND CARING PERSON.
I'M LOYAL AND TRUSTWORTHY.

your **THINKING SELF** will still come up with negative counter-argument: this always happens.

WHAT ABOUT *THAT* TIME?
YOU DON'T *ALWAYS* KEEP SECRETS.

EXERCISE

Repeat the following statements to yourself and notice what thoughts pop into your head in response:

I am a human being.

I am a worthwhile human being.

I am a lovable, worthwhile human being.

I am a competent, lovable, worthwhile human being.

I am a perfect, competent, lovable, worthwhile human being.

YEAH, *RIGHT*!
WHO ARE YOU *KIDDING*?
STOP TALKING *RUBBISH*!
YOU *WISH*!
WHAT A JOKE!

Did you find the more POSITIVE the affirmation, the more NEGATIVELY your mind responded? Now let's REVERSE it and see what happens:

I AM A USELESS, WORTHLESS, UNVALUED PIECE OF HUMAN GARBAGE.
HANG ON A MINUTE: I'M NOT THAT BAD! NO WAY – I DON'T BELIEVE THAT!

The reality is we can waste a lot of time locked in this never-ending battle which is often FIERCE.

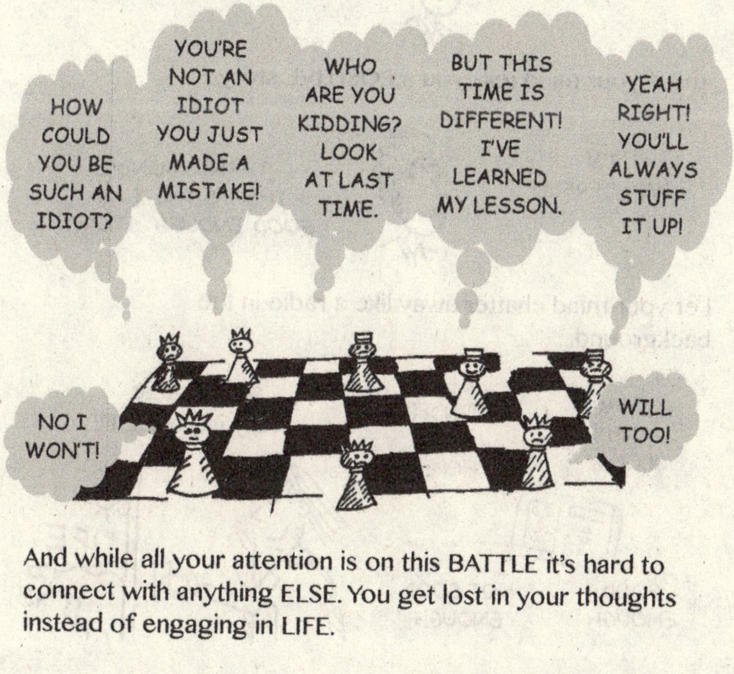
HOW COULD YOU BE SUCH AN IDIOT?
YOU'RE NOT AN IDIOT YOU JUST MADE A MISTAKE!
WHO ARE YOU KIDDING? LOOK AT LAST TIME.
BUT THIS TIME IS DIFFERENT! I'VE LEARNED MY LESSON.
YEAH RIGHT! YOU'LL ALWAYS STUFF IT UP!
NO I WON'T!
WILL TOO!

And while all your attention is on this BATTLE it's hard to connect with anything ELSE. You get lost in your thoughts instead of engaging in LIFE.

SO WHAT TO *DO*?
LEARN HOW TO BE LIKE THE CHESS BOARD.THE BOARD HOLDS THE PIECES BUT IT DOESN'T GET INVOLVED IN THE *BATTLE*!
HOW DO I DO THAT?
DEFUSION! UNHOOK YOURSELF FROM ALL THE STORIES — BOTH POSITIVE AND NEGATIVE. IF YOUR MIND TELLS YOU A NEGATIVE STORY, TRY THIS...

I'M A LOSER.
THANKS MIND! THERE'S THE '*I'M NOT GOOD ENOUGH*' STORY.

And if your mind tells you a POSITIVE story...

I'M WONDERFUL!
THANKS MIND! THERE'S THE '*I AM GOOD ENOUGH*' STORY!

Let your mind chatter away like a radio in the background...

DOOM AND GLOOM
WONDER AND HOPE
GOOD ENOUGH
NOT GOOD ENOUGH

...and engage fully in your LIFE.

LIFE

After all, at your funeral, would you want your loved ones to be thinking something like this...

SHE WAS SO CARING AND LOVING AND KIND AND GENUINE.
RIP

...or this?

SHE HAD A REALLY HIGH OPINION OF HERSELF.
RIP

You are not who you think you are. So unhook from the story, and get PRESENT!

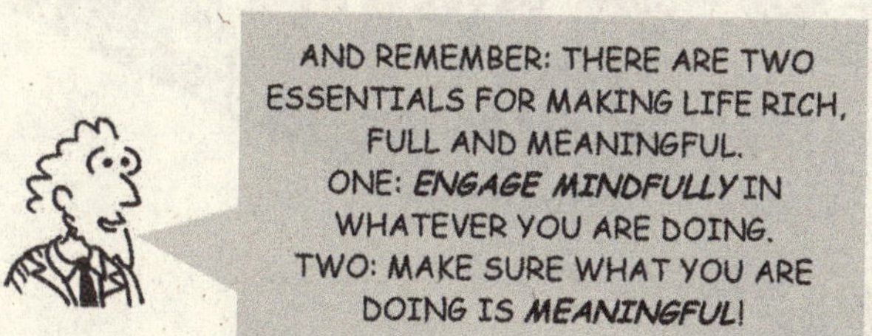
AND REMEMBER: THERE ARE TWO ESSENTIALS FOR MAKING LIFE RICH, FULL AND MEANINGFUL. ONE: ***ENGAGE MINDFULLY*** IN WHATEVER YOU ARE DOING. TWO: MAKE SURE WHAT YOU ARE DOING IS ***MEANINGFUL***!

I KNOW HOW TO DO THE FIRST ONE, BUT HOW DO I DO THE SECOND?
YOU'LL FIND OUT IN THE NEXT PART OF THE BOOK.

Chapter 12

Follow your heart

WHAT'S LIFE ALL ABOUT?
WHAT AM I HERE FOR?
WHAT MAKES LIFE WORTH LIVING?

In order to create a rich, full and meaningful life, it's important to reflect on WHAT WE'RE DOING and WHY WE'RE DOING IT.

It's time to ask some BIG QUESTIONS in order to clarify your VALUES.

- What is deeply important to you?
- What sort of person do you want to be?
- What sort of relationships do you want to build?
- If you weren't struggling with feelings and avoiding fears what would you channel your time and energy into doing?

VALUES are:

- our heart's deepest desires for how we want to behave, and what we stand for in life
- how we want to treat ourselves, others and the world around us.

When we live guided by values, we gain vitality and we experience life as RICH, FULL and MEANINGFUL – yes, even when it HURTS.

VALUES are not the same as GOALS.

VALUE

I WANT TO BE *LOVING* AND *CARING.*

GOAL

I WANT TO GET *MARRIED.*

VALUE

- How you want to behave, deep in your heart.
- A direction you want to keep moving in.
- An ongoing process with no end.

GOAL

- Something you want to get, complete, have, own, or achieve.
- Once achieved, it's over and done with; completed; 'ticked off the list'.

GOAL	**GOAL COMPLETED**	**WITH ONGOING VALUES**	**WITHOUT ONGOING VALUES**

I WANT *A BETTER JOB.*
YOU'RE *HIRED.*
I WANT TO BE *PRODUCTIVE, CREATIVE,* AND *RESPONSIBLE.*
I'LL SHOW UP TILL *HOME TIME.*

WHY ARE VALUES SO IMPORTANT?
LET ME INTRODUCE THE JEWISH PSYCHIATRIST VIKTOR FRANKL.

FRANKL SURVIVED AUSCHWITZ ...
AND LATER WROTE ...
MAN'S SEARCH FOR MEANING
... BASED ON HIS EXPERIENCES & OBSERVATIONS IN THE CAMP
IN PARTICULAR HE NOTICED THAT THOSE WHO SURVIVED THE LONGEST WERE OFTEN NOT THE FITTEST OR STRONGEST ...
... BUT THOSE WHO HELD A SENSE OF PURPOSE &
MY CHILDREN!
I'LL TELL THIS TO THE WORLD!
AND SOMETHING TO LIVE FOR!
FRANKL'S PURPOSE WAS HIS WIFE
I'LL KEEP GOING FOR HER!
I'LL SEE HER AGAIN!
AND HIS VALUES GAVE HIM MEANING EVEN THROUGH THE HORRORS
HOLD ON JOSEF!
WHILE THOSE WITHOUT LOST THE WILL TO LIVE!

Life can be HARD WORK. Anything meaningful brings CHALLENGES. Often this leads us to give up or quit.

IT'S TOO HARD.
I'M NOT EVEN GOING THERE!

VALUES make the EFFORT worthwhile.

If your values are:

CONNECTING WITH NATURE

...you'll make the trek.

BEING A LOVING PARENT

...you'll make time to play with your kids.

SELF-CARE

...you'll exercise and eat well.

But what if (like so many, not just those who are depressed) you think:

WHAT'S THE *POINT*?
IS THAT *ALL* THERE IS?
I HAVE *NOTHING* TO OFFER.
SOMETIMES I DON'T WANT TO *LIVE* ANYMORE.

Even THEN, values can give your life PURPOSE and MEANING.

EXERCISE

Imagine that you're 80 years old.

Now finish the following sentences:

- I spent too much time worrying about...
- I spent too little time doing things such as...
- If I could go back in time I would...

NOW NOTICE – ARE THOSE *DEMONS* COMING BACK ON THE DECK OF THE BOAT?
YES!

THOUGHT DEMONS	FEELING DEMONS
I'm a hypocrite!	Anxiety
I'll fail!	Confusion
It's too late!	Guilt
I can't change!	Frustration
I'm too busy!	Fear
I'm too tired!	Shame
I shouldn't have to!	Regret
	Embarrassment

SO DROP ANCHOR!
HOW?

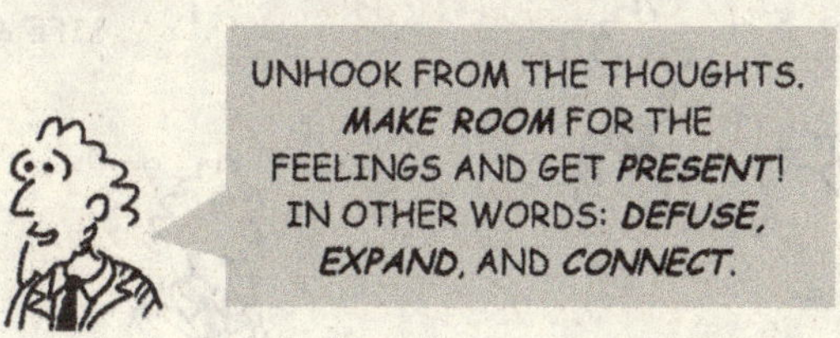
UNHOOK FROM THE THOUGHTS. *MAKE ROOM* FOR THE FEELINGS AND GET *PRESENT*! IN OTHER WORDS: *DEFUSE*, *EXPAND*, AND *CONNECT*.

What do you really WANT?

TO BE HAPPY
TO BE RICH
TO BE SUCCESSFUL
A GREAT JOB
SOMEONE TO LOVE ME
TO MARRY AND HAVE KIDS

These answers are not VALUES – they are all GOALS. To help you clarify VALUES, please do the exercise in the next chapter.

And remember: the PAST doesn't exist – it's just MEMORIES in the PRESENT...

...and the FUTURE doesn't exist either – it's just THOUGHTS and IMAGES in the PRESENT.

SO WHAT DOES THAT LEAVE YOU WITH?
NOW!
SO REMEMBER...
...LIFE GIVES MOST TO THOSE WHO MAKE THE MOST OF WHAT LIFE GIVES!

Chapter 13

The 1000-mile journey

We're going to start this chapter a little differently to all the others: no cartoons, just an exercise on clarifying your values. Please complete it before reading the rest of the book; it's very important for everything that follows later.

EXERCISE: CLARIFY YOUR VALUES

Below are 40 of the most common values. Please read through the list and write a letter next to each value, based on how important it is to you:

V = very important
Q = quite important
N = not important

1. Acceptance/self-acceptance: to be accepting of myself, others, life, etc. ☐
2. Adventure: to be adventurous; to actively explore novel or stimulating experiences ☐
3. Assertiveness: to respectfully stand up for my rights and request what I want ☐
4. Authenticity: to be authentic, genuine, and real; to be true to myself ☐
5. Caring/self-care: to be caring toward myself, others, the environment, etc. ☐
6. Compassion/self-compassion: to act kindly toward myself and others in pain ☐
7. Connection: to engage fully in whatever I'm doing and be fully present with others ☐

8. Contribution and generosity: to contribute, give, help, assist or share
9. Cooperation: to be cooperative and collaborative with others
10. Courage: to be courageous or brave; to persist in the face of fear, threat or difficulty
11. Creativity: to be creative or innovative
12. Curiosity: to be curious, open-minded, and interested; to explore and discover
13. Encouragement: to encourage and reward behaviour that I value in myself or others
14. Excitement: to seek, create and engage in activities that are exciting or stimulating
15. Fairness and justice: to be fair and just to myself or others
16. Fitness: to maintain or improve or look after my physical and mental health
17. Flexibility: to adjust and adapt readily to changing circumstances
18. Freedom and independence: to choose how I live and help others do likewise
19. Friendliness: to be friendly, companionable or agreeable toward others

20. Forgiveness/self-forgiveness: to be forgiving toward myself or others ☐

21. Fun and humour: to be fun loving; to seek, create and engage in fun-filled activities ☐

22. Gratitude: to be grateful for and appreciative of myself, others and life ☐

23. Honesty: to be honest, truthful and sincere with myself and others ☐

24. Industry: to be industrious, hardworking and dedicated ☐

25. Intimacy: to open up, reveal and share myself, emotionally or physically ☐

26. Kindness: to be kind, considerate, nurturing, or caring toward myself or others ☐

27. Love: to act lovingly or affectionately toward myself or others ☐

28. Mindfulness: to be open to, engaged in and curious about the present moment ☐

29. Order: to be orderly and organised ☐

30. Persistence and commitment: to continue resolutely, despite problems or difficulties ☐

31. Respect/self-respect: to treat myself and others with care and consideration ☐

32. Responsibility: to be responsible and accountable for my actions ☐

33. Safety and protection: to secure, protect or ensure my own safety or that of others ☐

34. Sensuality and pleasure: to create or enjoy pleasurable and sensual experiences ☐

35. Sexuality: to explore or express my sexuality ☐

36. Skilfulness: to continually practise and improve my skills and apply myself fully ☐

37. Supportiveness: to be supportive, helpful and available to myself or others ☐

38. Trust: to be trustworthy; to be loyal, faithful, sincere and reliable ☐

39. Other: ....
....
.... ☐

40. Other: ....
....
.... ☐

Adapted from *The Confidence Gap: From Fear to Freedom*, by Russ Harris, published by Penguin Group (Australia), Camberwell, 2010.

SO I'VE IDENTIFIED MY *VALUES* — *NOW WHAT?*
NOW YOU NEED TO TAKE *ACTION*! A MEANINGFUL LIFE DOESN'T JUST *HAPPEN* — YOU NEED TO *MAKE* IT HAPPEN!
LET'S BEGIN BY DIVIDING YOUR LIFE INTO *FOUR DOMAINS*:

1. HEALTH

Includes physical health, psychological health, spiritual health.

2. LEISURE

Includes fun and games — relaxation, sports, hobbies, creativity.

3. WORK/EDUCATION

Includes unpaid work (e.g. volunteering) and apprenticeships and self-education (e.g. reading books).

4. RELATIONSHIPS

Includes friends, family, neighbours, co-workers, etc.

NOTE: Start with one domain at a time or you'll get overwhelmed and give up. Over time, you can work through all of them.

SO HOW DO I START?
THERE ARE FIVE STEPS IN SETTING MEANINGFUL GOALS:

STEP 1: SUMMARISE YOUR VALUES

Write down four or five of the most important values in this domain...

IN MY RELATIONSHIP WITH MY WIFE MY VALUES ARE LOVE, CARING, HONESTY AND SUPPORT.
HEALTH – MY VALUES ARE SELF-ENCOURAGEMENT AND SELF-COMPASSION.

STEP 2: SET AN IMMEDIATE GOAL

Boost your confidence by starting with a SMALL, EASY goal – one that can be accomplished TODAY!

BE SPECIFIC

I'LL RING MY WIFE AND TELL HER I LOVE HER.
I'LL WALK FOR 10 MINUTES AT LUNCHTIME.
I'LL COOK A HEALTHY DINNER.

Remember: the journey of 1000 miles begins with a single step!

STEP 3: SET SOME SHORT-TERM GOALS

What are some small things you can do over the coming days or weeks that are consistent with your values?

I LIKE HELPING OTHERS BUT THIS JOB DOESN'T ALLOW IT...
...SO I'LL SEARCH THE INTERNET FOR A MORE MEANINGFUL JOB.

Remember: lots of small steps ADD UP.

STEP 4: SET SOME MEDIUM-TERM GOALS

Now stretch yourself a bit further.
Remember: be SPECIFIC.

I VALUE TAKING CARE OF MY BODY — I'LL JOIN A GYM BY THE END OF THE MONTH.
I'LL COOK HEALTHY RECIPES THREE NIGHTS A WEEK.
I'LL TAKE A 20 MINUTE WALK EVERY DAY.

STEP 5: SET SOME LONG-TERM GOALS

WHAT CHALLENGES WILL TAKE ME IN MY *VALUED DIRECTION*?
WHAT WOULD I LIKE TO DO IN THE NEXT 6 MONTHS, 1 YEAR, 5 YEARS, ETC?

ACTION PLANS

Now break down your goals into an action plan.

- What smaller steps are required to complete this?
- What resources do I need?
- When, specifically, will I carry out these actions?

If your goal is to go to the gym three times a week your ACTION PLAN might be to:

Join the gym

Get your gear together

Plan the times you'll go

The RESOURCES you might need may be:

Money for membership...

...gym gear

...and a bag to put this in.

Being SPECIFIC may involve:

I'LL PACK MY BAG *NOW.*
I'LL JOIN *STRAIGHT AFTER WORK.*
AND I'LL DO MY FIRST SESSION *THERE* AND *THEN*!
GYM

BUT WHAT IF I DON'T HAVE THE *RESOURCES*?

You can:

- **change your goal**

I COULD GO RUNNING — IT'S *FREE*!

- **make an ACTION PLAN to obtain the resources.**

I'LL *SAVE UP*!

Sometimes a resource is a SKILL:

MY GOAL IS
TO IMPROVE
RELATIONSHIPS
BUT I DON'T
KNOW *HOW*!

You can:

- **plan how you will learn the skill**
- **research/read, etc**
- **take a course.**

EXERCISE

Write down:

- a domain of life to work on
- your values in that domain
- goals (immediate, short, medium, long-term)
- your action plan for the immediate and short-term goals.

The GOOD NEWS is...

THE MOMENT YOU START STEERING
TOWARDS THE SHORE YOU'RE NO LONGER
DRIFTING ALL AT SEA AND YOU CAN
MAKE THE MOST OF THE JOURNEY ALONG
THE WAY KNOWING YOU'RE FINALLY
HEADING IN THE *RIGHT DIRECTION*!

Chapter 14

Finding fulfilment

IN A VALUES-FOCUSED LIFE YOU'RE MORE LIKELY TO ACHIEVE YOUR GOALS.
WHY?
BECAUSE IF YOUR GOALS ARE IN LINE WITH YOUR VALUES, YOU'RE MORE MOTIVATED TO PURSUE THEM!
PLUS — CONNECTING WITH AND ACTING ON YOUR VALUES CAN GIVE YOU FULFILMENT RIGHT NOW.
IN WHAT WAY?
SAY YOU WANT TO BUY A HOUSE — THAT'S YOUR GOAL — BUT YOU CAN'T AFFORD IT YET. WHY WOULD YOU PURSUE THAT GOAL?
TO PROVIDE SECURITY AND TAKE CARE OF MY FAMILY.
SO TAKING CARE OF THE FAMILY IS THE CORE VALUE HERE, YES?
YES.
WELL YOU CAN TAKE CARE OF YOUR FAMILY ANYWAY!
I SEE! I CAN STILL LIVE TO MY VALUES WHETHER OR NOT I GET THE HOUSE!

IF YOU BELIEVE YOU CAN'T BE HAPPY TILL YOU'VE ACHIEVED YOUR GOAL, LIFE WILL BE MISERABLE!
BUT I REALLY WANT THE HOUSE!
YOU DON'T HAVE TO GIVE UP ON YOUR GOAL! START SAVING!
SO I DON'T HAVE TO WAIT TILL I GET THE HOUSE TO HAVE THE SATISFACTION OF CARING FOR MY FAMILY.

Let's look at some other examples:

I WANT TO BE A DOCTOR BUT IT'S TEN YEARS OF HARD SLOG!
I'LL BE ABLE TO HELP PEOPLE!

What is the CORE VALUE of that GOAL?

There are many ways you can do that RIGHT NOW!

A common GOAL is to find a PARTNER...

SIGH, I'M LONELY!

...and to be MISERABLE if you HAVEN'T!

So what is the
CORE VALUE here?

TO BE *LOVING, CARING, SENSUAL* AND *FUN*!

You can still act on those values with FAMILY, FRIENDS — and YOURSELF.

BUT THAT'S NOT THE *SAME*!

No it's not, but you have a CHOICE...

- to find meaning, here and now, in living by your values or
- to be miserable by focusing on a goal you haven't achieved yet.

WHAT IF I *ACHIEVE* MY GOAL?
THERE'LL ALWAYS BE *SOMETHING ELSE* YOU WANT!

If you're always FOCUSED on GOALS, you will NEVER be content. However, your VALUES are ALWAYS available.

Chapter 15

A life of plenty

A beneficial by-product of creating a meaningful life is that POSITIVE EXPERIENCES will happen.

ISN'T THAT A *GOOD* THING?
OF COURSE — AND IT MAKES SENSE TO APPRECIATE THESE THINGS TO THE FULLEST WHILE YOU'RE EXPERIENCING THEM...
...BUT MAKING THEM THE MAIN *GOAL* IN LIFE IS NOT HELPFUL.
HOW COME?

Because you'll end up back in the HAPPINESS TRAP!

The more you focus on having only PLEASANT FEELINGS...

...the more you'll STRUGGLE against the UNPLEASANT ones.

THEN WHAT SHOULD I *DO* ABOUT *PLEASANT* FEELINGS?
BRING *MINDFULNESS* TO THEM!
EVERY DAY IS FULL OF OPPORTUNITIES TO *APPRECIATE* YOUR LIFE, EVEN WHILE YOU'RE *IMPROVING* IT!
BUT WE USUALLY DON'T EVEN *NOTICE* THESE THINGS.
WITH *MINDFULNESS* YOU CAN WAKE UP & EXPERIENCE ALL AROUND YOU!
HOW DO I DO *THAT*?
HERE ARE SOME WAYS...

When you EAT, slow down and SAVOUR it.

TASTE it. Feel the SENSATIONS in your mouth.

If it RAINS, pay ATTENTION to it.

Hear the PITCH and VOLUME. Watch the PATTERNS it makes. SMELL the air.

When it's SUNNY, APPRECIATE it.

FEEL its WARMTH on your skin. See how everything BRIGHTENS.

When you hug, kiss or shake hands with someone, ENGAGE in it.

Notice how it feels. Let WARMTH and OPENNESS flow through you.

When you feel good, SAVOUR it.

Notice how it feels in your BODY. Notice all the SENSATIONS, THOUGHTS and IMAGES. APPRECIATE it.

Look into the eyes of a person you care about as if for the FIRST TIME.

OBSERVE everything about them – GESTURES, MOVEMENT, FEATURES.

Observe an ANIMAL with childlike CURIOSITY.

See its COLOURS, MOVEMENTS, CONTOURS.

Take a familiar object and STUDY it as if you'd never seen such a thing before.

Use all your SENSES, appreciate its FUNCTION.

Before you get out of bed take TEN DEEP BREATHS.

Notice the MOVEMENT of your lungs and feel wonder at how they give you LIFE.

As you connect with your values and act in accordance with them you may notice changes in OTHERS, too.

The more you act like the person you WANT TO BE...

...the more you'll notice POSITIVE RESPONSES toward you.

ENJOY these responses. Be MINDFUL. Notice what is happening and APPRECIATE it.

When you act with OPENNESS, KINDNESS and ACCEPTANCE you'll probably receive the same...

...MOST of the time!

(If not, go elsewhere!)

Savour POSITIVE INTERACTIONS and notice the ABUNDANCE in your life.

Build the CONNECTIONS by:

EXPRESSING what you appreciate about others, life and yourself;

SHARING your difficulties and rewards;

LETTING OTHERS KNOW what they mean to you.

I LIKE THE WAY YOU DO THAT.

CAN I TELL YOU ABOUT...?

YOU'RE SUCH A *GOOD FRIEND*!

When you achieve goals that are in line with your values, there's often a pleasant emotion. Notice how it feels and ENJOY it – even the simple things.

THERE! IT'S *TIDY*.

A NICE, *HEALTHY* DINNER!

JUST A NOTE TO SAY HI!

It's all too easy to miss these things when the THINKING SELF tries to distract you with STORIES.

NOT GOOD ENOUGH!

MINDFULNESS

- awakens you to good things you may have taken for granted
- cultivates an attitude of openness and curiosity
- helps you to notice more opportunities
- provides stimulation and interest
- improves relationships
- increases fulfilment
- enables effective action.

NATURALLY IT'S EASIER TO BE MINDFUL WHEN LIFE IS GOING SMOOTHLY.
IN THE TOUGH TIMES, YOUR THOUGHTS WILL KEEP TRYING TO PULL YOU OFF COURSE.
THE IMPORTANT THING IS TO REMEMBER TO PRACTISE IT!
AND KEEP CATCHING MYSELF WHEN I GO OFF TRACK!

Chapter 16

Willingness

Say you've decided to climb a mountain because of the SPECTACULAR VIEW at the top.

Halfway up it's STEEP, NARROW and ROCKY.

You're COLD, TIRED and WET...

...and you know it will only get WORSE.

I DIDN'T THINK IT WOULD BE *THIS* HARD!

But you're WILLING to endure this discomfort not because you WANT it or ENJOY it but because it's on the way to where you WANT to GO.

I'LL HAVE THE *SATISFACTION* OF MAKING IT AND SEEING THOSE *GREAT VIEWS*!

And say you want to write a book – you'll encounter many OBSTACLES...

FUSION WITH UNPLEASANT THOUGHTS AND FEELINGS

I'LL NEVER SUCCEED.
I'M NOT *GOOD ENOUGH*.
WHAT IF I *FAIL*?
I FEEL *SCARED*.

PROCRASTINATION AND PUTTING OFF or **AVOIDANCE AND DISTRACTION**

THERE'S NO HURRY.
DEADLINE 1 WEEK!

I CAN'T THINK ABOUT IT NOW.
I NEED A DRINK.

You might finally TAKE ACTION

OKAY — I'LL SET A MANAGEABLE GOAL.
WRITE 10 PAGES
DAY

...and give it MEANING...

WHAT ARE MY *VALUES* BEHIND THIS GOAL?
• CHALLENGING SELF
• HELPING OTHERS
• BEING CREATIVE

...and acknowledge that no matter the outcome the effort will be WORTHWHILE.

JUST DOING THIS WILL EXPAND MY SKILLS.

But now you're down to the NITTY GRITTY and it's getting HARDER.

I'M *BLOCKED.*

You may be tempted to BAIL OUT...

I'M REALLY NOT *ENJOYING* THIS!

...that's where WILLINGNESS comes in.

BUT I'LL *KEEP GOING*!

WILLINGNESS MEANS

- making room for unpleasant thoughts and feelings in order to do something meaningful
- getting out of your comfort zone to do something you value.

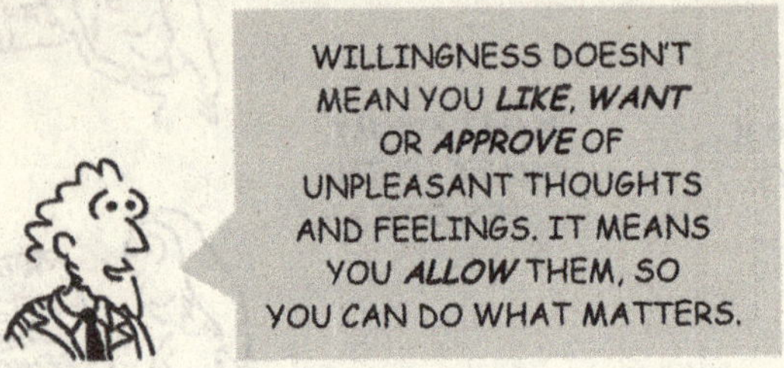
WILLINGNESS DOESN'T MEAN YOU *LIKE, WANT* OR *APPROVE* OF UNPLEASANT THOUGHTS AND FEELINGS. IT MEANS YOU *ALLOW* THEM, SO YOU CAN DO WHAT MATTERS.

Willingness is something we practise in small ways every day...

WHAT *THOUGHTS, FEELINGS, SENSATIONS* AND *URGES* AM I WILLING TO HAVE IN ORDER TO DO WHAT I *VALUE*?

To enjoy a movie you're willing to PAY for the ticket.

To go on holiday you are willing to PACK.

TIRED!

To pass an exam you're willing to STUDY.

Willingness is the only way to deal with OBSTACLES. When an obstacle presents itself you can say:

NO!

and your life stays stuck or gets smaller...

OR

YES!

in which case there's no guarantee that life will get easier...

or that there won't be another tougher or bigger obstacle down the road!

But by saying YES your life will get BIGGER.

HOW WILL MY LIFE *EXPAND* IF I STILL KEEP MEETING OBSTACLES?
BY SAYING YES YOU GAIN *EXPERIENCE* AND *INNER STRENGTH*. YOU *GROW* AS A PERSON!

If FINDING A PARTNER is important to you, along the way you'll experience:

And you might have some real DISAPPOINTMENTS!

Either you're WILLING to go through this or you're NOT.

You might want to change to a more MEANINGFUL JOB...

which might mean:

- less pay
- years of extra study
- parental disapproval.

But if you're WILLING you might reach your goal.

EXERCISE

Make a list of what you are willing to experience in order to reach your goal.

Now ask yourself:

THOUGHTS
CAN'T DO THIS
TOO HARD
FEELINGS
ANXIETY
BOREDOM
SENSATIONS
RACING HEART
TIGHT JAW
URGES
RUN AWAY
EAT
ARE THERE ANY OF THESE I CAN'T *HANDLE*?
NO!

(provided you practise EXPANSION DEFUSION and CONNECTION)

WHAT WOULD BE USEFUL *REMINDERS*?
FAMOUS QUOTES
WHAT'S THE *SMALLEST*, *EASIEST* STEP I CAN BEGIN WITH?
SEARCH NET

AND *WHEN* WILL I BEGIN?
NOW!

Chapter 17

A meaningful life

You can apply the ***ACT*** principles to ANY area of your life you'd like to improve:

HEALTH

LEISURE

WORK/ EDUCATION

RELATIONSHIPS

Whatever you're doing, ENGAGE FULLY with it.

Whoever you're with be FULLY PRESENT for them.

When unhelpful thoughts arise DEFUSE them.

Whenever unpleasant feelings arise MAKE ROOM for them.

And whatever your values are be FAITHFUL to them.

THE *ACT* SERENITY CHALLENGE

Develop the courage to solve those problems that can be solved, the serenity to accept those problems that can't be solved and the wisdom to know the difference.

Adapted from the 'Serenity Prayer'

If your problems CAN be solved...

SHORT
OF CASH

...take EFFECTIVE ACTION in line with your values.

If they CAN'T be solved...

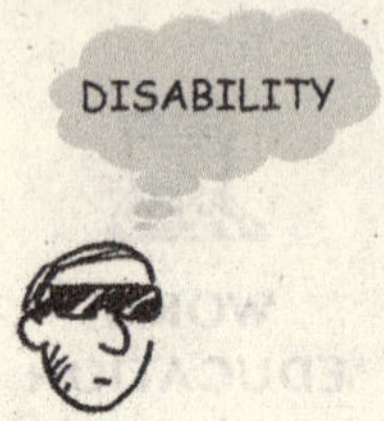
DISABILITY

...use DEFUSION, EXPANSION and CONNECTION to help you ACCEPT this.

And be sure to practise CONNECTION.

FOCUS *HERE*
AND *NOW*

You can either **ACCEPT** *or* **take EFFECTIVE ACTION** *or* **do both simultaneously**.

And as you take action, ENGAGE FULLY in what you're doing. Act on your VALUES and pay attention to the effect your actions are having.

Remember, too: the PAST doesn't exist; it's just MEMORIES in the PRESENT. And the FUTURE doesn't exist; it's just THOUGHTS in the PRESENT.

SO WHAT DOES THAT LEAVE YOU WITH?
NOW!
REMEMBER: LIFE *GIVES MOST* TO THOSE WHO MAKE THE *MOST* OF WHAT LIFE *GIVES*!